What Is Python Good For?

Anna Novikova

Table of Contents

Introduction

When you only start to learn programming, you get acquainted with one or two programming languages and use them for all your tasks just because you don't have any other choice. But when you learn a few programming languages more, you start to understand that their application areas are often different. It is not about syntax or object-oriented paradigm vs. functional paradigm or strong typing vs. weak typing (however all things are also important). But if you need to build a mobile application for iOS or a website or a business application with complex database logic or a real-time application - your (or your company's) choice of a programming language will probably be different for these cases and it is quite normal since there is no silver bullet.

So imagine you know or have just found out by googling that Python is a high-level general-purpose dynamically typed multi-paradigm language. Fine - but when can it be really useful? In what areas you may apply it easily and successfully? These are the questions we will try to answer throughout this book.

I hope this book will be useful for different readers with different programming backgrounds. It can be used even by absolute beginners who learn Python as their first programming language. I hope for beginners this book will be inspiring because you will see that complex purposes can be reached with the help of simple-to-use Python tools. I am not going to explain the details of Python syntax or the basics of Python programming but I will try to give some references (books or tutorials) in each chapter. If Python is still a complete mystery for you I advise you to read books [1] and [2] first and then return to this book. If you are a beginner, I advise you to study Coursera's Python for Everybody specialization [3] by Dr. Chuck (Charles Russell Severance).

As for seasoned Python developers, they probably know most of the stuff but I hope at least chapters about GPT-3 API, OpenCV, machine and deep learning will be useful for them.

But when I think about the main audience of this book, I imagine experienced but non-Pythonic enough developers like C# developers, Java developers and C++ developers. I am mostly a C# developer so probably I wouldn't use Python for a cross-platform desktop application which should have a nice interface or file parsing, there are great means for doing this by .NET/C# tools. But I believe for web scraping or deep learning or plots Python is much more convenient compared to C#. So easy-to-use Python tools can be suitable for a problematic area of another language.

In the areas of machine learning and deep learning Python is a unique tool to get results relatively quickly (yes, I know about R but I don't think it is as convenient and rich as Python) so even if your main language is different, you should definitely try Python for these areas that are so popular and widely used now.

Each chapter gives a different use case for Python so they can be read in any order. But please note that the first chapters are easier use cases and the last ones are more difficult. Feel free to skip a chapter if you are not interested in its topic, each chapter can be read separately from others.

Sure you can just read the book but if you would like to get the most from it, it is better first to read a chapter and then launch the samples and try to modify them according to your needs. All code samples can be found on GitHub.

https://github.com/anovik/what-is-python-good-for

You are welcome to use all the samples for your own purposes, their license is MIT. But please remember they are just examples and not the real industrial code. Their aim is to show concepts and not to deal with all possible situations. So you probably need to add at least exception handling to use them in real-life projects.

In the scope of this book I create my samples using Python 3.10. To execute them you should install any Python 3.x version, this should be sufficient in most cases. It is absolutely fine to use the latest Python 3.x version.

If you use Python 2, this is up to you to adapt the samples due to syntax and library differences between Python 2 and Python 3. Since Python 2 support was officially terminated in 2020, many libraries stopped supporting Python 2 as well. This way if you still want to use Python 2, you will sometimes need to install older library versions and maybe change the sample syntax.

All Python code in the samples is cross-platform so you are welcome to use your favorite OS.

The easiest way to work with samples is to clone the GitHub repository above, open the folder with the chapter you are reading, and launch .py files in your favorite IDE or just use the command line/terminal.

Notation

Here is a brief explanation of my notation used throughout the book.

[7] - this is a book or tutorial or website number from References

>pip install beautifulsoup4

This means I am going to install some Python library or package (I use these two words as synonyms throughout this book) to run the next piece of code. If you are going to also run the sample, you need to install the same library. You can do it using pip like I do for my samples or you can use Anaconda if this is more convenient for you.

The code samples or their outputs are marked with bold font:

```
response = requests.get(
    url="https://en.wikipedia.org/wiki/Python_(programming_language)",
)
```

Chapter 1. Web Scraping

Web scraping is a process of extracting and analyzing data from various websites. This can be easy or difficult or even impossible due to legal issues or various methods to prevent web scraping.

Python has a great package named BeautifulSoup which makes this process easier. You can install it with a command:

>pip install beautifulsoup4

Also, we need requests Python package. It is a simple Python library that allows easy handling of HTTP requests.

>pip install requests

Now we can do some Wikipedia scraping. Our task will be to take a Wikipedia article about Python 3

https://en.wikipedia.org/wiki/Python_(programming_language)

and scrape some information from it like titles or links.

The page looks like this:

We need to import our two libraries:

import requests
from bs4 import BeautifulSoup

First we need to do an HTTP GET request to get the content of the HTML page by its URL:

```python
response = requests.get(
    url="https://en.wikipedia.org/wiki/Python_(programming_language)",
)
```

The content of the HTML page is stored in a Python object called **response** and we create a BeautifulSoup object feeding this **response** object to it:

soup = BeautifulSoup(response.content, 'html.parser')

Let's briefly discuss the structure of any HTML document, we will need this information for future parsing. HTML (Hypertext Markup Language) is a standard markup language for webpages. Here is a very simple HTML example:

```html
<!DOCTYPE html>
<html>
<head>
<style>
#myHeader {
  background-color: blue;
  color: black;
  text-align: center;
}

.header {
  background-color: blue;
  color: black;
}
</style>
</head>
<body>

<h1 id="myHeader">Main Header</h1>

<h2 class="header">Section 1</h2>

<h2 class="header">Section 2</h2>

<a href="https://www.google.com/">Would you like to google something?</a>

<img src="test.jpg">

</body>
</html>
```

Any HTML page consists of HTML elements. Any HTML element has a start tag, some content (maybe empty) and an end tag. HTML elements can have attributes that provide some additional information. In our example, **id**, **class**, **href** and **src** are HTML attributes. The **id** attribute specifies the id for an HTML element and must be unique within a given HTML document. It is used for access to this element and to specify a style declaration for it. On the contrary, the **class** attribute can be used by many HTML elements and is often used for specifying a class name in the style sheet.

The power of BeautifulSoup is in the easy finding of elements or tags by their id, CSS class, attribute value, etc. To start with let's find the main header of the page by its id (you can always check this id by manually looking at the HTML page source in the browser):

```python
title = soup.find(id="firstHeading")
print(title.text)
```

This piece of code gives us the following string:

Python (programming language)

This is correct. Now let's proceed with a more complex task, get the list of hyperlinks that our page contains (usually there are many of them so we will print the first 10 hyperlinks).

```python
allLinks = soup.find(id="bodyContent").find_all("a")
[print(link.get('href')) for link in allLinks[:10]]
```

What is actually going on here? **find()** returns the first matching HTML tag, in this case it is the first HTML tag with an id equal to **bodyContent** (this is the main area of the wiki page so we hope there is only one such tag actually). Then we get the list of all hyperlinks that this bodyContent tag contains with the help of **find_all()**. And the last step is just printing the **href** attribute value for the first 10 hyperlinks. This gives us the following output:

```
/wiki/Wikipedia:Protection_policy#semi
/wiki/File:Wiki_letter_w.svg
/wiki/Wikipedia:Manual_of_Style/Lead_section#Length
/wiki/Wikipedia:Summary_style
/wiki/Wikipedia:Manual_of_Style/Lead_section#Provide_an_accessible_overview
/wiki/File:Python-logo-notext.svg
/wiki/Programming_paradigm
/wiki/Multi-paradigm_programming_language
/wiki/Object-oriented_programming
#cite_note-1
```

Note that in real-life situations this list may be empty. Generally speaking, in practice we should devote much more attention to the processing of possible errors or unexpected situations (for example, no links have been found or even the main area doesn't exist with the id we expect - because webpages often change). We ignore most of these possible problems in our samples because our main task is to show scraping concepts and error processing is a separate huge topic.

If we don't need to get the list of all hyperlinks for a tag, we can get just the first link of the tag, in our case a tag with an id equal to **bodyContent**. We will do it using a CSS selector. CSS selectors allow the identification of HTML elements as targets for CSS styles. BeautifulSoup provides functions **select()** and **select_one()** for selecting elements specifying a CSS selector. Soup Sieve package is used by BeautifulSoup, it is another great library for selecting, matching, and filtering elements using powerful and modern CSS selectors.

```
firstLink = soup.select_one("#bodyContent a")
print(firstLink.get('href'))
```

It prints:

/wiki/Wikipedia:Protection_policy#semi

select_one() returns the first tag that matches the specified criteria. With the help of the CSS selector **"#bodyContent a"** we ask for the first hyperlink of **#bodyContent** main area of the page. **id="bodyContent"** and **#bodyContent** are equivalent (search by id and CSS selector respectively).

Similarly but using **select()** instead of **select_one()** which returns all the tags matching the specified criteria we can print the hyperlink number 20 or any other number (we assume that our list is long enough):

```
anotherLink = soup.select("#bodyContent a")[20]
print(anotherLink.get('href'))
```

It gives us the following output:

/wiki/Software_release_life_cycle

CSS selectors may be the most convenient way of finding the elements because using them simplifies testing and future changes in the code. If you put CSS selectors to variables and re-use them, it will be easier to deal with them (comparing to id or attributes) in case the page has changed or even you need to migrate to another scraping library.

OK, we have found some tags by id or CSS selector, now let's try to find tags by their class. We will print section headers (see the left side of our wiki page screenshot).

```
sections = soup.find_all("span", class_="mw-headline")
[print(section.text) for section in sections]
```

History
Design philosophy and features
Syntax and semantics

In this chapter we have briefly discussed how to use BeautifulSoup for web scraping. It is really powerful for HTML tags search by CSS selector, id, class, etc. But please keep in mind that for real scrapers or scraping bots you need to check also other possible issues (legal issues, possible anti-bot or anti-crawler protection).

If you are interested in the topic of web scraping using Python, I advise you to read the book [4].

Chapter 2. File Parsing

Python may be useful for different file formats parsing and conversion. Let's briefly cover a couple of examples.

XML and JSON

Our first task in this chapter will be to create an XML(which stands for Extensible Markup Language, widely used for storing data) file and then convert it to JSON (Javascript Object Notation) file.

Let's first create a simple XML file, there are many options for this - including ElementTree, cElementTree and LXML. The most popular option is ElementTree which has been included in the standard Python library since Python 2.5. Here is the code for creating a simple XML file:

```python
import xml.etree.cElementTree as ET

root = ET.Element("root")
ET.SubElement(root, "introduction")
book = ET.SubElement(root, "book")

ET.SubElement(book, "chapter1", name="Python For Beginners",
pagesnumber="100").text = "Would you like to learn some Python?"
ET.SubElement(book, "chapter2", name="Advanced Python",
pagesnumber="300").text = "Let's go deeper!"
ET.SubElement(book, "chapter3", name="More Advanced Python",
pagesnumber="1000").text = "Now you can write your own version of GPT-10."

tree = ET.ElementTree(root)

ET.indent(tree, space="\t", level=0)

tree.write("output.xml", encoding="utf-8")
```

What is going on here? We simply add arbitrary elements and subelements one by one. For each subelement we may set various attributes. **ET.indent()** function allows us to generate pretty-printed XML output and then we just write all the tree to a file named output.xml to keep things simple. It is also worth noting that **ET.indent()** function is available for Python 3.9+ but you can easily replace it for older versions of Python (for example, using xml.dom.minidom).

Let's launch our Python file and we should get a file in the same directory called output.xml with the following content:

```xml
<root>
   <introduction />
   <book>
        <chapter1 name="Python For Beginners" pagesnumber="100">Would you like to learn some Python?</chapter1>
        <chapter2 name="Advanced Python" pagesnumber="300">Let's go deeper!</chapter2>
        <chapter3 name="More Advanced Python" pagesnumber="1000">Now you can write your own version of GPT-10.</chapter3>
   </book>
</root>
```

Now our aim is to take this XML as input and convert it to JSON. Make sure you've installed xmltodict Python module:

```
>pip install xmltodict
```

And here is the code:

```python
import xmltodict
import json

with open("output.xml") as xml_file:
        parsedDict = xmltodict.parse(xml_file.read(), attr_prefix=', cdata_key='text')

json = json.dumps(parsedDict, indent=1)

with open("output.json", "w") as json_file:
        json_file.write(json)
```

xmltodict.parse() parses provided XML input and converts it to the dictionary doing all the preliminary work. Then we serialize this dictionary to JSON string (indent allows us to do the pretty-printing, this is the same thing we did for XML before) and write this string to output.json file.

Here is the content of output.json:

```json
{
 "root": {
  "introduction": null,
  "book": {
   "chapter1": {
        "name": "Python For Beginners",
        "pagesnumber": "100",
        "text": "Would you like to learn some Python?"
   },
   "chapter2": {
```

```json
        "name": "Advanced Python",
        "pagesnumber": "300",
        "text": "Let's go deeper!"
    },
    "chapter3": {
        "name": "More Advanced Python",
        "pagesnumber": "1000",
        "text": "Now you can write your own version of GPT-10."
    }
  }
 }
}
```

And finally, let's zip our JSON file. Zip is a common format for archives and compression. Python has zipfile module to easily create, read and write zip files.

```python
from zipfile import ZipFile

with ZipFile('output.zip', 'w') as zipFile:
    zipFile.write('output.json')
```

So with just three lines of code we get output.zip archive with output.json inside.

Images

Now let's check how you can work with images using Python. Imagine we have a bunch of JPEG files and would like to make their size a little bit smaller without losing too much quality. This may be the case for you if you have some good-quality images or photos having large file sizes and you would like to upload them to your website.

For image processing we will use Python Imaging Library (PIL). It is a great library supporting different image formats. PIL allows opening and saving files as well as different image processing operations like changing color or brightness, adding text to images, and applying various filters.

We will install a version that supports Python 3:

```
>pip install Pillow
```

Let's do the import of libraries in our Python file:

```python
import os
from PIL import Image
```

And define a function that will do the main job - compress a JPEG file:

```python
def compressJpeg(file):
    filepath = os.path.join(os.getcwd(),
                    file)

    print(os.path.getsize(filepath))

    picture = Image.open(filepath)

    picture.save("compressed_" + file,
            "JPEG",
            optimize = True,
            quality = 80)

    newFilePath = os.path.join(os.getcwd(),
                    "compressed_" + file)

    print(os.path.getsize(newFilePath))
    return
```

This function works with a file from the current directory. Its name is provided as an argument. We get the size of the provided file and print it (certainly, this step is optional, it is just only for results tracking). Then we open the file with PIL and save it with a reduced size.

The quality of the output image is set by **quality** parameter, here it is 80. It varies from 1 (the worst) to 95 (the best). Other values should be avoided, 95 means preserving initial quality. The default is 75. The better quality we have, the smaller the compression degree and vice versa.

After saving the new compressed JPEG, we print its size (also for tracking purposes).

Let's make our program compress all the JPEG files in its working directory. The idea here is to list all the files, filter them by extension, and call our compression function for JPEG files:

```python
currentdir = os.getcwd()

formats = ('.jpg', '.jpeg')

for file in os.listdir(currentdir):
    if os.path.splitext(file)[1].lower() in formats:
        compressJpeg(file)
```

If I run the program with an arbitrary JPEG file, I receive the results like this:

```
6124478
4380244
```

These numbers are input and output file sizes. So we easily reduced the JPEG from 6 MB to 4 MB. You can play with **quality** parameter to get the desired result for your files.

Another way to reduce the image size is resizing it to a given width or height maintaining its aspect ratio - instead of compression. Let's define the function **resizeJpeg** similar to our previous function **compressJpeg**:

```python
import os
import PIL
from PIL import Image

def resizeJpeg(file):
    filepath = os.path.join(os.getcwd(),
                file)

    print(os.path.getsize(filepath))

    picture = Image.open(filepath)

    resizedHeight = 500

    hpercent = (resizedHeight / float(picture.size[1]))
    newWidth = int((float(picture.size[0])*float(hpercent)))
    img = picture.resize((newWidth, resizedHeight), Image.LANCZOS)

    img.save("resized_" + file)

    newFilePath = os.path.join(os.getcwd(),
                "resized_" + file)

    print(os.path.getsize(newFilePath))
    return
```

Here instead of reducing image quality we resize it to given height = 500, calculating a new width so the aspect ratio was the same. You can set the height to any number you need.

Let's call the function for JPEG files in the current directory:

```python
currentdir = os.getcwd()

formats = ('.jpg', '.jpeg')

for file in os.listdir(currentdir):
    if os.path.splitext(file)[1].lower() in formats:
        resizeJpeg(file)
```

For the same image we get the following sizes:

6124478
71462

Similarly you use fixed width instead of fixed height - in this case, you need to calculate a new height.

This method can help to reduce image filesize a lot which can be really useful for web pages.

Chapter 3. Working with Various APIs

API (Application Programming Interface) is a way or protocol defining how different programs can interact with each other. Python is a great tool for dealing with almost every REST (Representational state transfer) API which is the most popular type of API protocol nowadays. It is easy to work with Twitter API, GitHub API and a lot of other APIs using Python.

Nowadays Generative pre-trained transformers (GPT) are really popular. The first GPT model was released in 2018 by OpenAI, an artificial intelligence company based in San Francisco, California. OpenAI released a sequence of these models called "GPT-n".

The latest and the most capable model is GPT-4. GPT-4 is a multimodal large language model (LLM), the exact number of the model parameters is unknown and it is not revealed by OpenAI. It was released in 2023 and for now is available upon request, you can register on the waitlist and OpenAI decides whether they will allow access to GPT-4 API for you depending on your aims and purposes.

For our samples, we will use GPT-3 API since it is easily available. GPT-3 API is open for public use. GPT-3 was released by OpenAI in 2020, its architecture is a decoder-only transformer network with a 2048-token-long context, has 175 billion parameters, requiring 800GB to store. So it is clear that it is NOT easy to train a similar model yourself, that's why most people have to rely on public API.

Let's try to use Python for playing with GPT-3. GPT-3 API has the official Python bindings which you can simply install:

>pip install openai

To run the samples and create your own ones, you need to register on the OpenAI API website and create your own API key here:

https://platform.openai.com/account/api-keys

It is highly advisable first to play with GPT-3 using OpenAI playground, it doesn't require any kind of programming at all (also it is great fun!) and only then continue with our samples and programming. Try it here:

https://platform.openai.com/playground

Now back to programming. First, we will import the necessary libraries:

import os
import openai

All requests to OpenAI API should include your own API key. Remember your API key is a secret, so it is advised to store it separately and not to add it to git or other version control systems. For example, Python can get the key from environmental variables:

```python
openai.api_key = os.getenv("OPENAI_API_KEY")
```

Alternatively, you can read it from another file or use a .env file.

And now we can finally do the actual job with GPT-3. We will use Completions API, with it you give the prompt and model returns predicted completion to your query. Our first prompt will be: "What is Python good for?" - because this is our main question in the scope of this book and we would like to know what GPT-3 thinks about it. So we ask for completion for this prompt:

```python
response = openai.Completion.create(
  model="text-davinci-003",
  max_tokens=256,
  prompt="What is Python good for?"
)
```

In addition to **prompt** we set the model name here, for our samples we use **text-davinci-003** which is not the fastest but it is considered to be the most capable of GPT-3 models. **max_tokens** is a parameter that limits the length of generated content.

After running this code we receive the following in response:

```json
{
  "id": "cmpl-7RlqxwUmP7t7LXGD6vsigZ9SuFXH0",
  "object": "text_completion",
  "created": 1686741683,
  "model": "text-davinci-003",
  "choices": [
    {
      "text": "\n\nPython is a general-purpose programming language that is widely used in a variety of applications, including web development, desktop applications, scripting, database programming, mobile applications, artificial intelligence, machine learning, and more. Python has gained popularity for its simplicity and readability, as well as for its large number of built-in libraries that make it easier to implement complex algorithms and problem-solving techniques. It is also used for creating games and graphical user interfaces. As an interpreted language, Python is agile and can be used for rapid prototyping and iterative development with fewer lines of code than other languages.",
      "index": 0,
      "logprobs": null,
      "finish_reason": "stop"
    }
  ],
```

```
  "usage": {
    "prompt_tokens": 6,
    "completion_tokens": 123,
    "total_tokens": 129
  }
}
```

To extract the actual response text only we can simply do the following:

print(response['choices'][0]['text'])

And here is what we get:

Python is good for performing web application development, data science and scientific computing, artificial intelligence and machine learning, scripting, automation, desktop app development, game development, and more. Python is a very versatile language with a growing community of developers.

Well, it is a quite good answer! It could be one of the initial paragraphs of this book. Now let's ask another question - What is Python bad for?

```
response = openai.Completion.create(
  model="text-davinci-003",
  max_tokens=256,
  prompt="What is Python bad for?"
)
```

print(response['choices'][0]['text'])

And this is the answer from GPT-3:

Python is not well-suited for mobile development and game development. It is also not great for applications that require a high level of performance, such as graphic-intensive applications or high-frequency trading. Additionally, Python's syntax can be overly complex and verbose, which can make it difficult to debug and maintain.

Again, this is a reasonable answer, no wonder students try using GPT-3 to pass their exams. But please note both answers are not perfect. For example, game development is mentioned both as a good and bad side of Python. Can you find other drawbacks in these two answers?

Now let's check if GPT-3 is capable of writing Python code. We will ask it to create some web scraping code (a task similar to our Chapter 1):

```
response = openai.Completion.create(
  model="text-davinci-003",
  max_tokens=256,
```

```python
    prompt="Create Python code for web scraping of wiki page"
)

print(response['choices'][0]['text'])
```

Here is the code written by GPT-3:

```python
from bs4 import BeautifulSoup
import requests

# URL of page to be scraped
URL = "https://en.wikipedia.org/wiki/Web_scraping"

# sending a get request to the URL
page = requests.get(URL)

# create a BeautifulSoup object from the HTML
soup = BeautifulSoup(page.content, "html.parser")

# extracting all the <p>Tags from the webpage
p_tags = soup.find_all("p")

# go through the paragraphs and print out the text
for p in p_tags:
    print(p.text)
```

The code is generally ok, it runs, necessary libraries are imported and it prints all the paragraphs for a given page. So GPT-3 is capable of solving easy programming tasks.

If you have access to GPT-4, you can try the same or other prompts with it. GPT-4 is more advanced and reliable and has much better capabilities with image processing so the results should be better generally.

It is worth mentioning that using GPT-3 API with Python bindings is really simple. And you can use other REST APIs in the same way.

Chapter 4. Creating Websites

Python is widely used in the modern world of web development. There are several popular web frameworks for Python including Django and Flask. In this chapter we will build a very basic website using Django. It will be a website about this book and its chapters.

Django is a very popular and powerful high-level web framework, written in Python. You can build any type of website using it.

Setting up the Django Project

It is recommended to have a dedicated virtual environment for each Django project so let's start from creating it. A virtual environment allows the handling of multiple Django projects on the same machine, each of these projects can have different dependencies (on Python versions and Python packages).

For creating our virtual environment we will use the built-in Python tool **venv**. Here are the commands for Windows and Unix/Mac OS which allow creating the virtual environment called **bookenv** (the name is completely arbitrary, choose whatever you like for your website):

>py -m venv bookenv

>python -m venv bookenv

Before installing Django and working on the actual website we need to activate our just created virtual environment, here are the activation commands for Windows and Unix/Mac OS respectively:

>bookenv\Scripts\activate.bat

>source bookenv/bin/activate

Similar commands can be used for deactivation of the virtual environment:

>bookenv\Scripts\deactivate.bat

>source bookenv/bin/deactivate

When you are in the virtual environment, your command prompt starts with

(bookenv)

So before you start working with Django you activate the virtual environment and after the work, you may deactivate your virtual environment. Each time you launch the command line prompt you need to activate the virtual environment once again. We assume that all the following commands in this chapter will be performed in our **bookenv** virtual environment.

Now we can install Django in it (don't forget to do this in our virtual environment):

>pip install Django

Now let's create the new project called **mybook** in the **bookenv** folder:

>django-admin startproject mybook

This command creates the initial structure of the project as follows:

```
mybook
    manage.py
    mybook/
        __init__.py
        asgi.py
        settings.py
        urls.py
        wsgi.py
```

Now let's go to mybook folder and create an app there (it is a web application which has some meaning in your Django project).

>py manage.py startapp chapters

This command creates **chapters** folder with initial files in it. Currently, we have the following structure:

```
mybook
    manage.py
    mybook/
    chapters/
        migrations/
            __init__.py
        __init__.py
        admin.py
        apps.py
        models.py
        tests.py
        views.py
```

All these files have their own specific meaning, for example, **views.py** is for views. Django views are Python functions that take an HTTP request and return an HTTP response. The simplest view ever we can create is to return a hard-coded string like "Hello world!":

from django.shortcuts import render

```python
from django.http import HttpResponse

def chapters(request):
    return HttpResponse("Hello world!")
```

To see the result from this view, we need to call the view through URL. For this purpose, let's create a file for **chapters** application - **urls.py** in the same folder as **views.py** with the following content:

```python
from django.urls import path
from . import views

urlpatterns = [
    path('chapters/', views.chapters, name='chapters'),
]
```

This file is responsible for URL management for **chapters** folder. But we need first to get here from **mybook** so we need to describe this action in **mybook/urls.py**. Initially, it looks like:

```python
from django.contrib import admin
from django.urls import path

urlpatterns = [
    path('admin/', admin.site.urls),
]
```

We need to add one line as follows:

```python
from django.contrib import admin
from django.urls import include, path

urlpatterns = [
    path('', include('chapters.urls')),
    path('admin/', admin.site.urls),
]
```

Now we can launch the server:

```
>py manage.py runserver
```

And check the result in a browser:

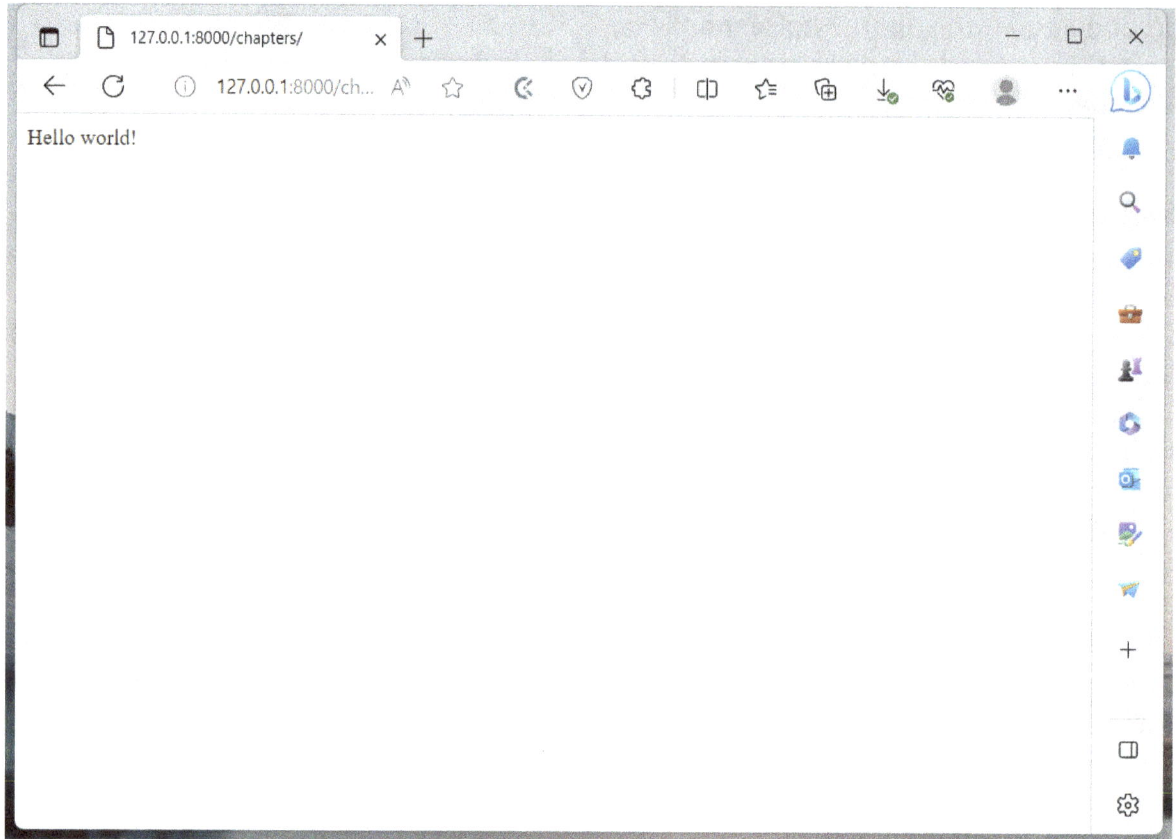

Now we can see that our mechanism of urls and views is working.

To go further we need to let Django know about our application. We should go to mybook/settings.py and add **chapters**:

INSTALLED_APPS = [
  'django.contrib.admin',
  'django.contrib.auth',
  'django.contrib.contenttypes',
  'django.contrib.sessions',
  'django.contrib.messages',
  'django.contrib.staticfiles',
  'chapters'
]

Let's apply the changes (we will discuss this command a little bit later together with other migrations commands):

>py manage.py migrate

We should get the following:

Operations to perform:
  Apply all migrations: admin, auth, contenttypes, sessions
Running migrations:

Applying contenttypes.0001_initial... OK
Applying auth.0001_initial... OK
Applying admin.0001_initial... OK
Applying admin.0002_logentry_remove_auto_add... OK
Applying admin.0003_logentry_add_action_flag_choices... OK
Applying contenttypes.0002_remove_content_type_name... OK
Applying auth.0002_alter_permission_name_max_length... OK
Applying auth.0003_alter_user_email_max_length... OK
Applying auth.0004_alter_user_username_opts... OK
Applying auth.0005_alter_user_last_login_null... OK
Applying auth.0006_require_contenttypes_0002... OK
Applying auth.0007_alter_validators_add_error_messages... OK
Applying auth.0008_alter_user_username_max_length... OK
Applying auth.0009_alter_user_last_name_max_length... OK
Applying auth.0010_alter_group_name_max_length... OK
Applying auth.0011_update_proxy_permissions... OK
Applying auth.0012_alter_user_first_name_max_length... OK
Applying sessions.0001_initial... OK

Working with Data

Until now, we have worked with static data and currently, we need to add real information about our book chapters, their names, descriptions, etc. In Django, the work with data is performed with the help of models. The models created in the Django project by default correspond to database tables. When we created our Django project, an empty SQLite database **db.sqlite3** was created in **mybook** folder so it will be used for data storage. SQLite seems to be a great solution for data storage at the beginning of the project and if later you feel it is not enough for your needs, it is easy to switch to PostgreSQL, MySQL, or Oracle which are also supported by Django.

We are going to add a model class called **Chapter** to **chapters/models.py** file:

from django.db import models

class Chapter(models.Model):
  name = models.CharField(max_length=255)
  description = models.TextField()

We add two fields to our model here, **name** and **description**. The first one is a **CharField**, which is intended for keeping small or medium-size strings and we specify its maximum length as 255 characters. The second one is a **TextField**, intended for storing large text, paragraphs of text, etc.

So we have defined the **Chapter** model class but the database table is not yet created. To have it created, let's run the following command from **bookenv/mybook** folder:

>py manage.py makemigrations chapters

This command creates migrations - they are a way to propagate changes made in the model in Django. Here is the output from this command:

Migrations for 'chapters':
chapters\migrations\0001_initial.py
- Create model Chapter

From the output, we learn that a new file **0001_initial.py** was created automatically in **migrations** folder. Here it is:

```python
from django.db import migrations, models

class Migration(migrations.Migration):

    initial = True

    dependencies = [
    ]

    operations = [
        migrations.CreateModel(
            name='Chapter',
            fields=[
                ('id', models.BigAutoField(auto_created=True, primary_key=True,
serialize=False, verbose_name='ID')),
                ('name', models.CharField(max_length=255)),
                ('description', models.TextField()),
            ],
        ),
    ]
```

We need another command to apply the new migrations:

>py manage.py migrate

Operations to perform:
Apply all migrations: admin, auth, chapters, contenttypes, sessions
Running migrations:
Applying chapters.0001_initial... OK

Great, so now migrations are applied and we have a **Chapter** table in the SQLite database and can proceed further with some data inserting. Let's launch the Python shell from our virtual environment:

>py manage.py shell

All the next commands will be executed from the Python shell (note **>>>** at the beginning of lines). Let's import **Chapter** model:

>>>from chapters.models import Chapter

And check whether there are any records in the database table **Chapter**:

>>>Chapter.objects.all()

The output is the following:

<QuerySet []>

A QuerySet is a collection of data from a database and this output means the database is currently empty. So let's create the first Chapter object with the given **name** and **description**:

>>> chapter1 = Chapter(name="Web Scraping", description="Web scraping is a process of extracting and analyzing data from various websites. This can be easy or difficult or even impossible due to legal issues or various methods to prevent web scraping.")

Now we can save it to the database (i.e. perform INSERT):

>>> chapter1.save()

Let's check what objects are in the database table now:

>>>Chapter.objects.all().values()

<QuerySet [{'id': 1, 'name': 'Web Scraping', 'description': 'Web scraping is a process of extracting and analyzing data from various websites. This can be easy or difficult or even impossible due to legal issues or various methods to prevent web scraping.'}]>

Everything goes nicely, we have just inserted the first Chapter object into the database table. Let's insert the rest of them and run again:

>>>Chapter.objects.all().values()

<QuerySet [{'id': 1, 'name': 'Web Scraping', 'description': 'Web scraping is a process of extracting and analyzing data from various websites. This can be easy or difficult or even impossible due to legal issues or various methods to prevent web scraping.'}, {'id': 2, 'name': 'File Parsing', 'description': 'Python may be useful for different file formats parsing and conversion. Let's briefly cover a couple of examples.'}, {'id': 3, 'name': 'Working with Various APIs', 'description': 'API (Application Programming Interface) is a way or protocol defining how different programs can interact with each other. Python is a great tool for dealing with almost every REST (Representational

state transfer) API which is the most popular type of API protocol nowadays. It is easy to work with Twitter API, GitHub API and a lot of other APIs using Python.'}, {'id': 4, 'name': 'Creating Websites', 'description': 'Python is widely used in the modern world of web development. There are several popular web frameworks for Python including Django and Flask. In this chapter we will build a very basic website using Django. It will be a website about this book and its chapters.'}, {'id': 5, 'name': 'Graphs and Data Visualization', 'description': 'It is really simple even for absolute beginners to draw plots using Python due to the great plotting library called Matplotlib. Matplotlib together with Numpy (another awesome Python library adding support for arrays and matrices) provides a power comparable to MATLAB which is itself a great computing platform for analyzing data. But Matplotlib is much simpler to use. Matplotlib has clear and full online documentation so I advise you to go to https://matplotlib.org and browse as many as possible examples there. Here we will discuss some types of graphs including pie and bar charts.'}, {'id': 6, 'name': 'OpenCV', 'description': 'OpenCV stands for Open Source Computer Vision library. It is easy to guess it mainly deals with computer vision but it has very powerful functionality having modules for image processing, video, camera, machine learning and much much more. OpenCV itself is written in C++ and it has bindings for several languages including Python.'}, {'id': 7, 'name': 'Machine Learning', 'description': 'Machine learning and deep learning are among the most popular topics related to computer science today. In this chapter we will briefly discuss machine learning and in the next chapter - deep learning. Machine learning is a very wide topic so we will concentrate only on some Python-related aspects of it.'}, {'id': 8, 'name': 'Deep Learning', 'description': 'Deep learning is a kind of machine learning which we discussed in Chapter 7. The word "deep" means that its architecture has multiple layers (including an input layer, hidden layers and an output layer).'}, {'id': 9, 'name': 'What Python is Not Good For', 'description': 'Throughout this book we have discussed what a great language Python is and how it could be used. But it has its own problems and disadvantages (as any other language, I believe). In this chapter, we will briefly talk about the areas where Python is not so good (or even bad or totally unsuitable).'}]>

We have added all nine chapters with their names and descriptions (note: id was added automatically). Certainly, we can update or delete data in a similar way. For example, if you need to modify the description of the third chapter, you can do something like this:

```
>>>from chapters.models import Chapter
>>> ch = Chapter.objects.all()[2]
>>> ch.description = "YOUR UPDATED DESCRIPTION HERE"
>>> ch.save()
```

After adding some data, let's display them on a web page. Let's add three web pages: a main page, a page with a chapter list, and a page that will show the details for each chapter. We will create HTML files in the **bookenv/mybook/chapters** folder. They all will use the same master template, let's call it master.html:

```
<!DOCTYPE html>
<html>
<head>
```

```html
  <title>{% block title %}{% endblock %}</title>
</head>
<body>

{% block content %}
{% endblock %}


</body>
</html>
```

Pay attention to Django **block** and **endblock** tags, they mean that this content will be replaced by actual web page content.

Here is the content of **main.html**. Note it extends the master template and specifies the replacement for block tags:

```html
{% extends "master.html" %}

{% block title %}
  What Is Python Good For?
{% endblock %}


{% block content %}
  <h1>What Is Python Good For?</h1>

  <h3>Chapters</h3>

  <p>See the list of the book's <a href="chapters/">chapters</a></p>

{% endblock %}
```

Now we can add the **all_chapters.html** that will show the list of chapter names and give the link to each chapter details:

```html
{% extends "master.html" %}

{% block title %}
  What Is Python Good For? The list of all chapters.
{% endblock %}


{% block content %}
  <h1>Chapters</h1>

  <ul>
    {% for x in allchapters %}
```

```html
    <li><a href="chapter/{{ x.id }}">{{ x.name }}</a></li>
  {% endfor %}
 </ul>
{% endblock %}
```

Here we have a new thing - Django for loop allowing to iterate through items of a list, array, etc.

```html
{% for x in some_collection %}
 <h3>{{ x }}</h3>
{% endfor %}
```

And now only chapter.html is left to add - here its content. We display the chapter name and description:

```html
{% extends "master.html" %}

{% block title %}
  Details about {{ currentchapter.name }}
{% endblock %}


{% block content %}
 <h1>{{ currentchapter.name }} </h1>

 <p>{{ currentchapter.description }}</p>

 <p>Back to <a href="/chapters">Chapters</a></p>

{% endblock %}
```

To make all these HTML pages work properly, we need two more things. First, we need to add some views to **chapters/views.py**:

```python
from django.http import HttpResponse
from django.template import loader
from .models import Chapter

def chapters(request):
  allchapters = Chapter.objects.all().values()
  template = loader.get_template('all_chapters.html')
  context = {
    'allchapters': allchapters,
  }
  return HttpResponse(template.render(context, request))
```

```python
def chapter(request, id):
  currentchapter = Chapter.objects.get(id=id)
  template = loader.get_template('chapter.html')
  context = {
    'currentchapter': currentchapter,
  }
  return HttpResponse(template.render(context, request))

def main(request):
  template = loader.get_template('main.html')
  return HttpResponse(template.render())
```

We have three views, one per web page. Also, we make some changes in chapters/views.py:

```python
from django.urls import path
from . import views

urlpatterns = [
    path('', views.main, name='main'),
    path('chapters/', views.chapters, name='chapters'),
    path('chapters/chapter/<int:id>', views.chapter, name='chapter'),
]
```

And that's it! Now let's start the server:

```
>py manage.py runserver
```

Now we can visit http://127.0.0.1:8000/ to check all three web pages:

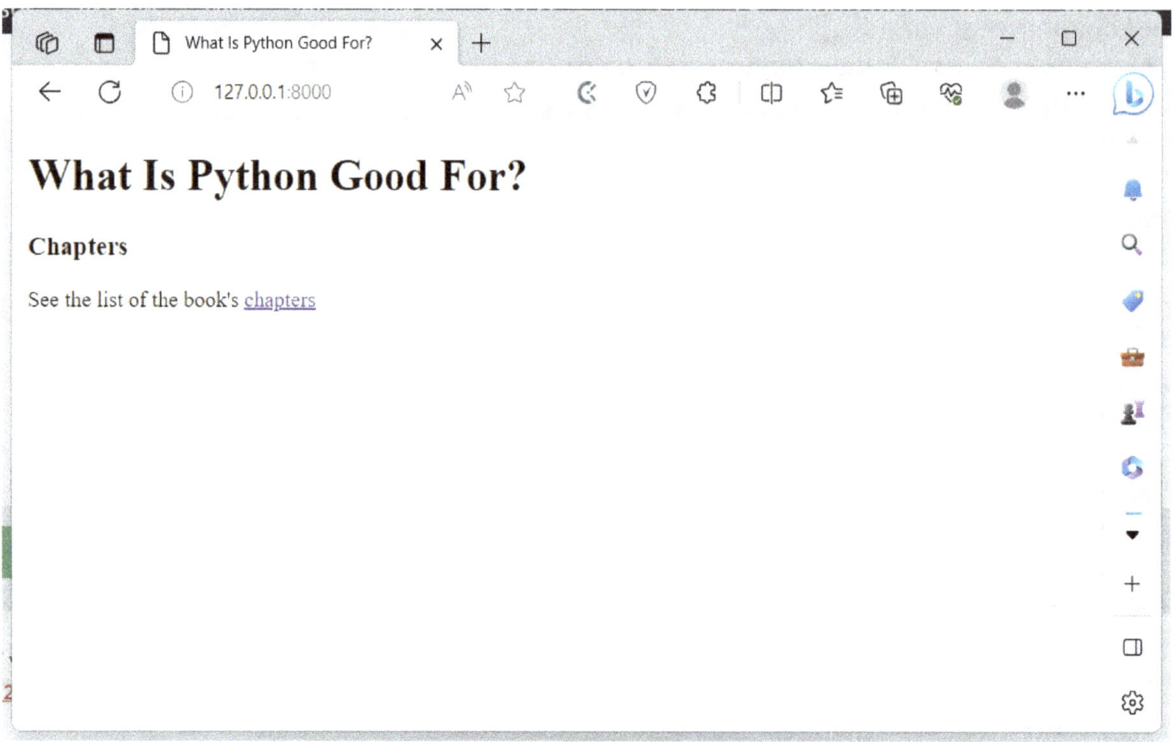

What Is Python Good For?
127.0.0.1:8000
What Is Python Good For?
Chapters
See the list of the book's chapters

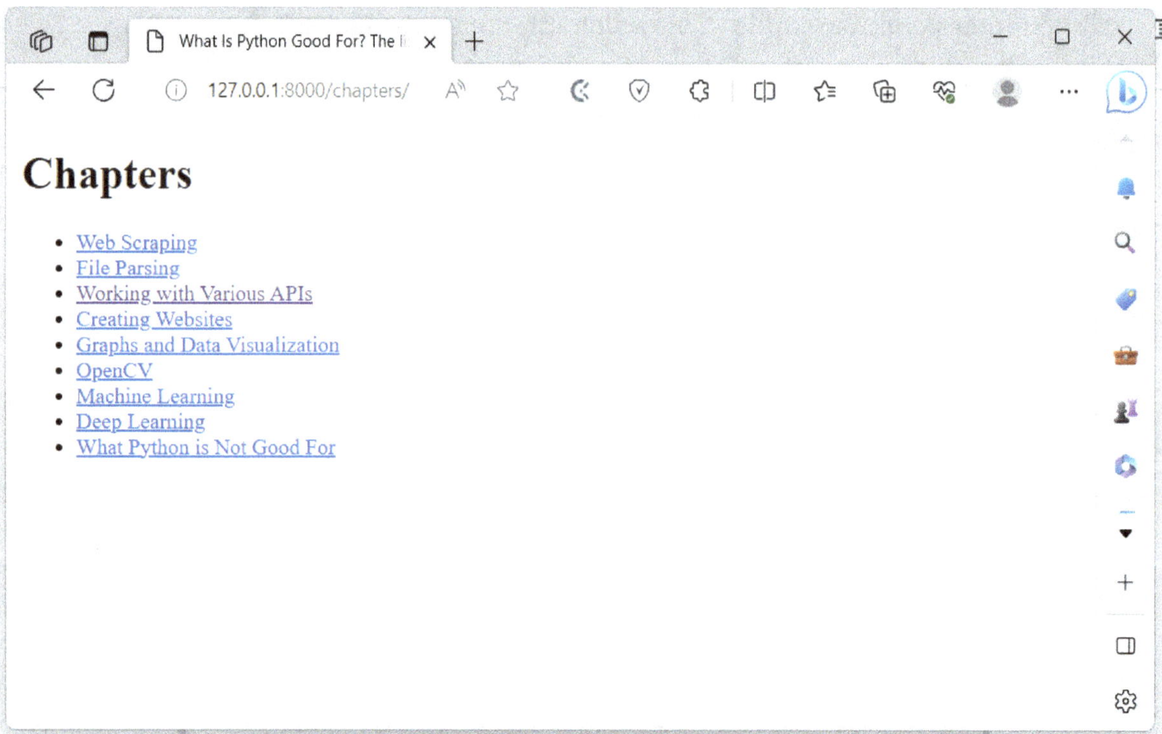

What Is Python Good For? The l
127.0.0.1:8000/chapters/
Chapters
Web Scraping
File Parsing
Working with Various APIs
Creating Websites
Graphs and Data Visualization
OpenCV
Machine Learning
Deep Learning
What Python is Not Good For

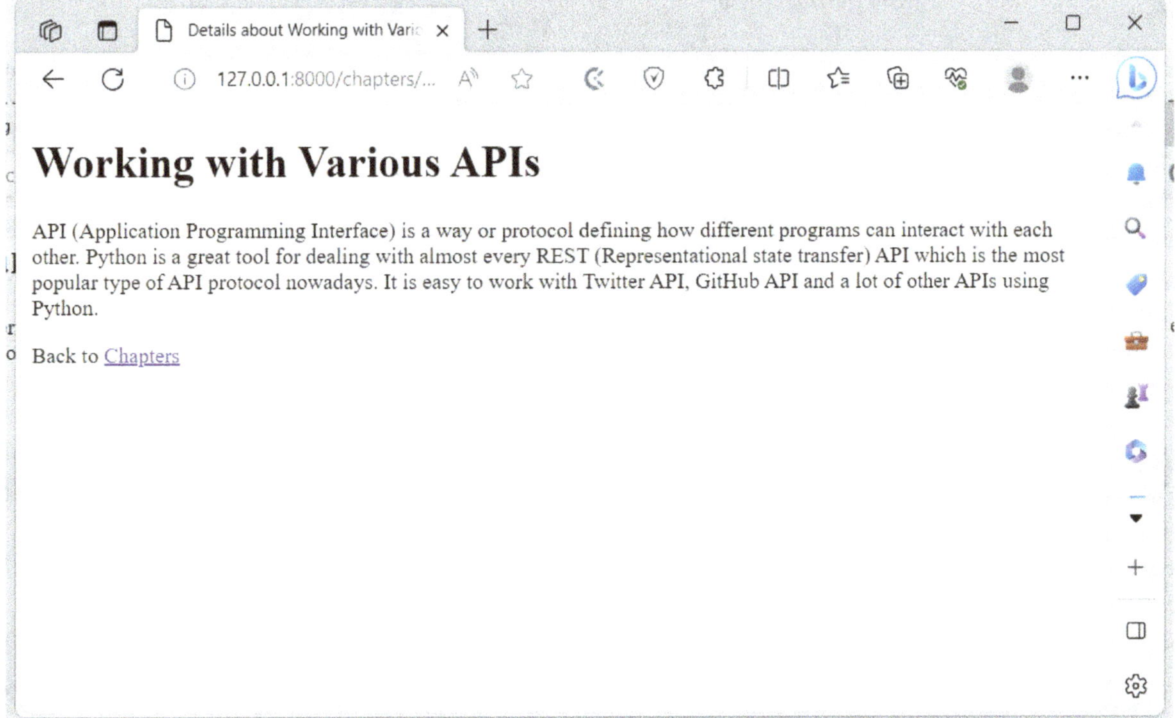

Great, our basic site is up and running!

Django Admin

Now let's look at Django Admin, it is a great built-in Django tool. It provides CRUD (stands for Create/Read/Update/Delete operations) for the models.

To launch Django Admin, navigate to **mybook** folder, and in the virtual environment execute the following command:

>py manage.py runserver

Now you can open the browser and go to http://127.0.0.1:8000/admin/

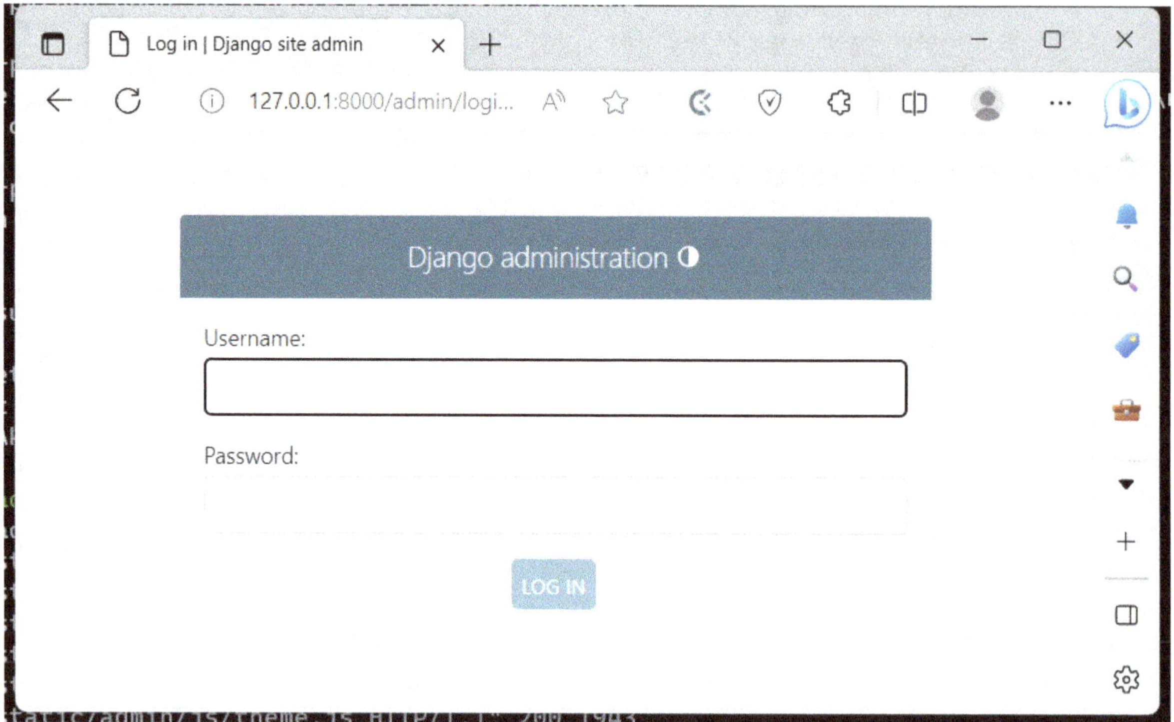

This is working because of **path('admin/', admin.site.urls),** in urls.py. **Admin/** gets redirected to the built-in Django application. Now we need to create a user to be able to log into Django Admin.

>py manage.py createsuperuser

This command will ask you about username, email address and password. Once this information is entered, you will receive the following message:

Superuser created successfully.

Now we can start the server again:

>py manage.py runserver

If we go to http://127.0.0.1:8000/admin/ link we can log into the admin account, providing the username and password we have just set.

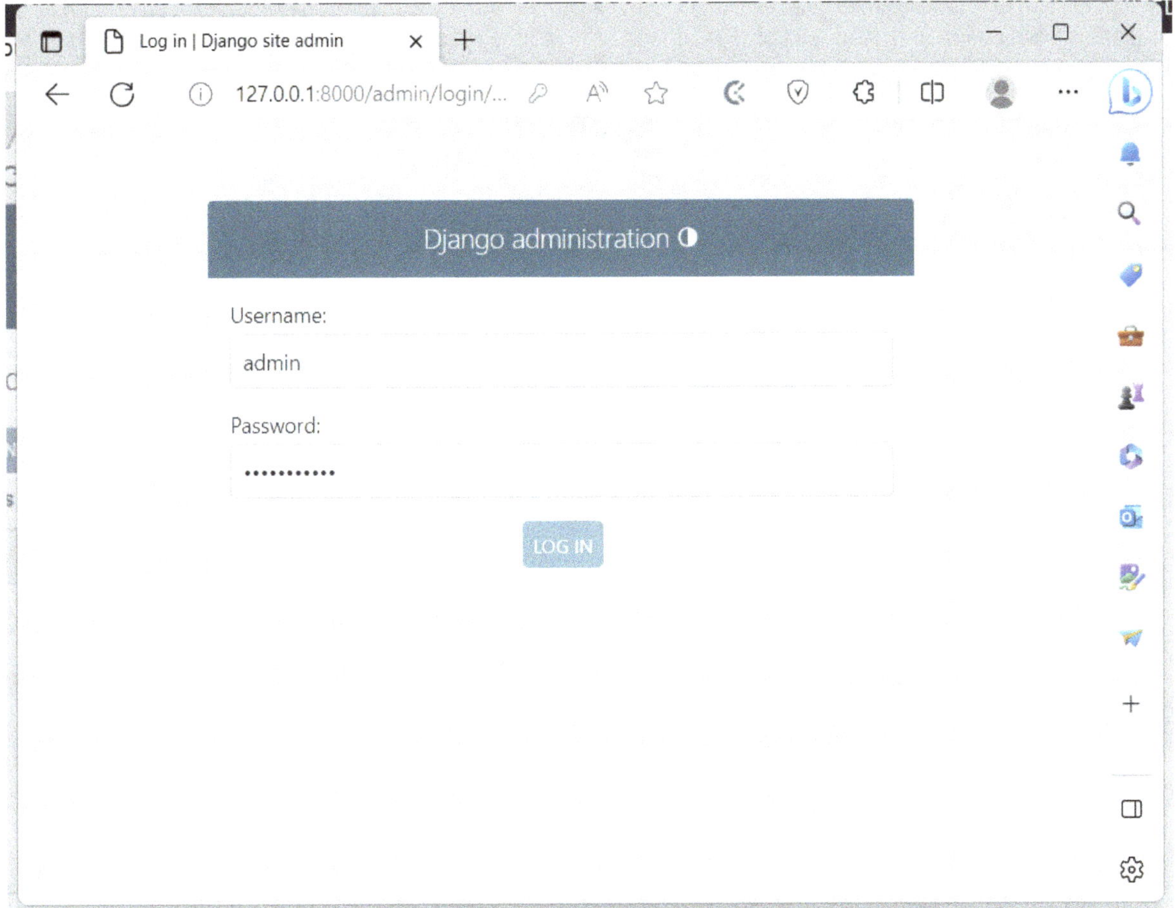

After logging in, we are redirected to the following screen where it is possible to do the CRUD operations for available models, but it seems there are no Chapters here?

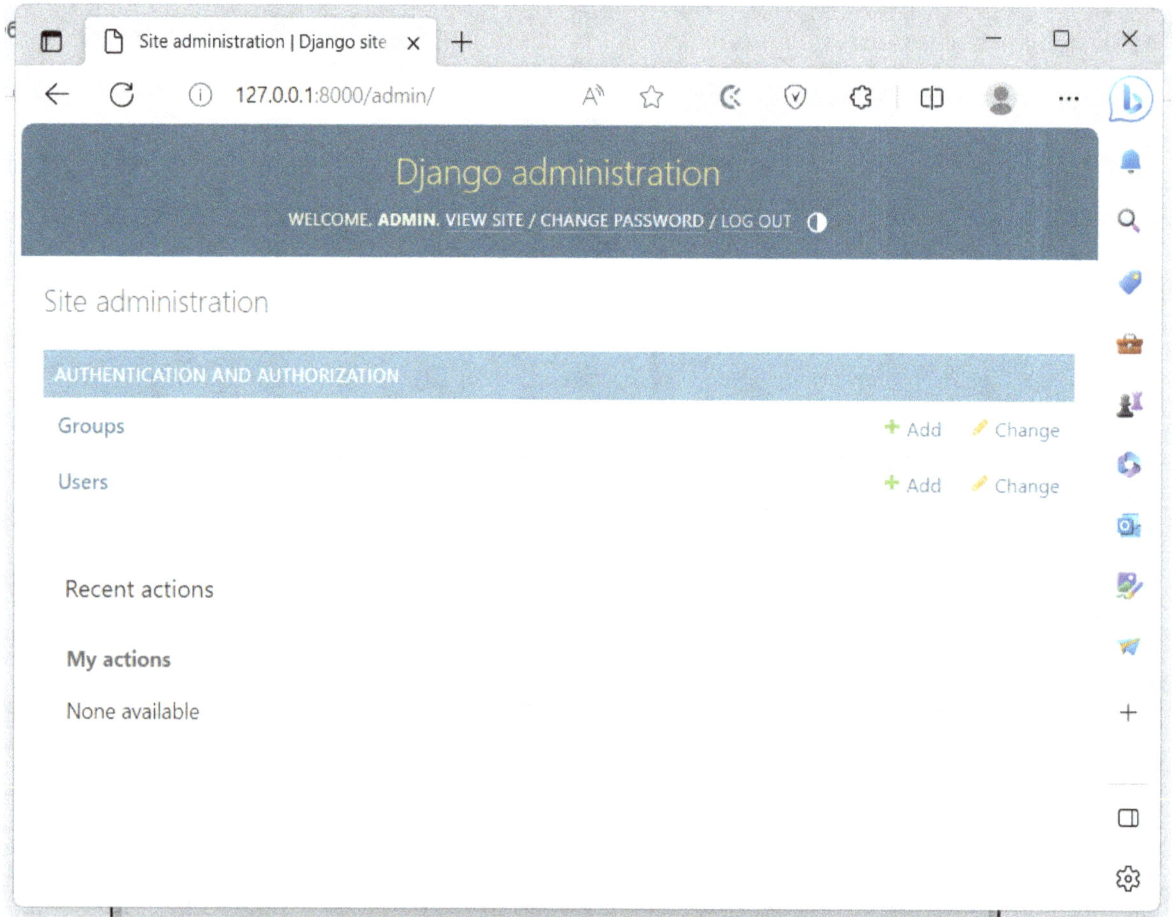

Now we need to open **mybook/chapters/admin.py** and add the following lines to it:

from .models import Chapter

 # Register your models here.
admin.site.register(Chapter)

And if you go now again to http://127.0.0.1:8000/admin/ we will see the Chapters and it is possible to add, update or delete them without any coding! All the information entered earlier with the Python shell is also here.

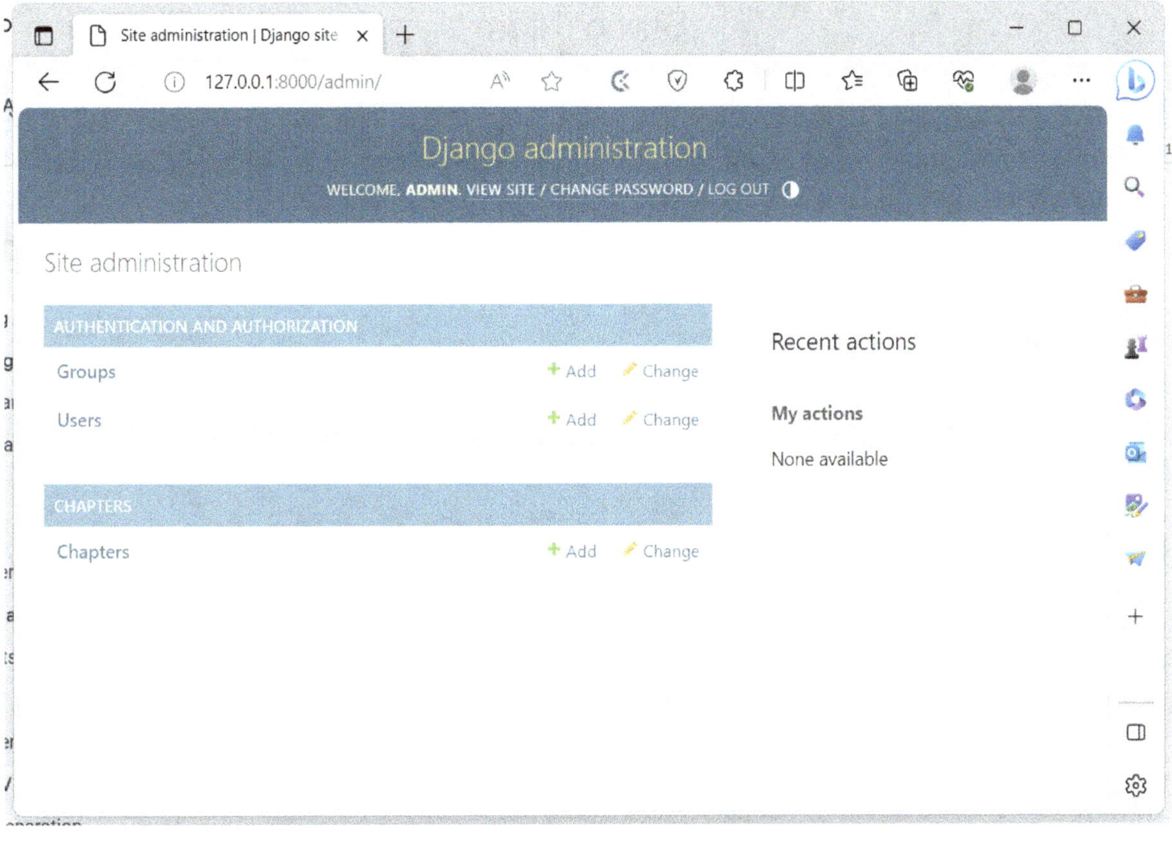

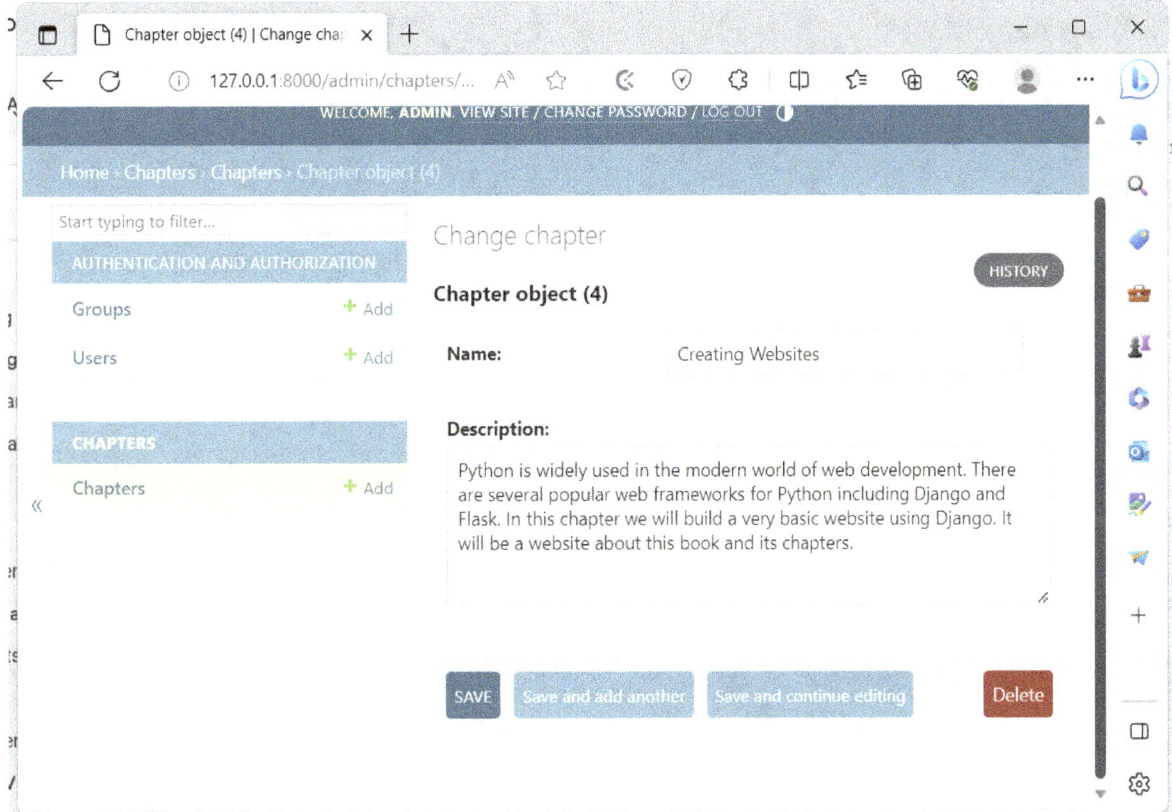

Static Files

Probably for each web application you will need to add static files like images or CSS files. Let's add a new folder **bookenv/mybook/chapters/static** and put a simple CSS file to it called **style.css** with the following content:

```css
body {
  background-color: lightblue;
  font-family: Arial, Helvetica, sans-serif;
}
```

Let's apply this CSS file in our master template:

```html
{% load static %}
<!DOCTYPE html>
<html>
<head>
  <title>{% block title %}{% endblock %}</title>
  <link rel="stylesheet" href="{% static 'style.css' %}">
</head>
<body>

{% block content %}
{% endblock %}

</body>
</html>
```

Now let's restart the server in the virtual environment and check the result in the browser:

```
>py manage.py runserver
```

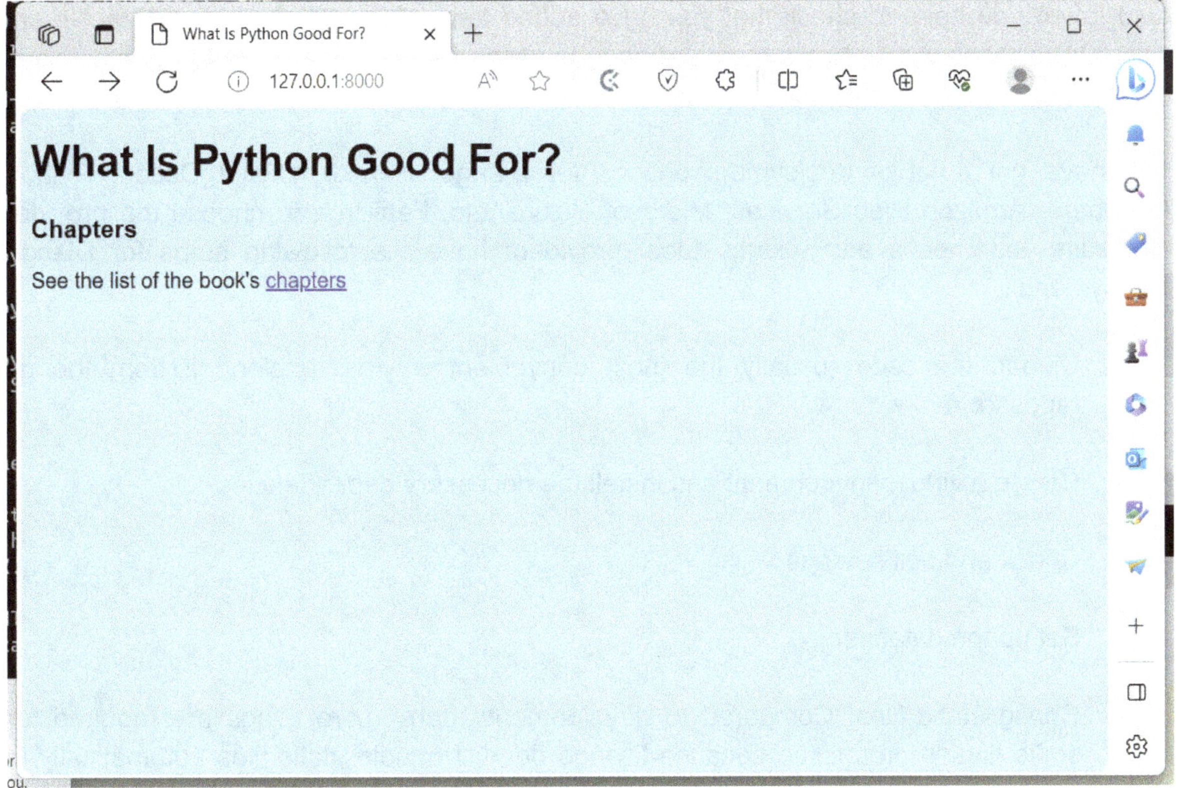

Warning: This should not be definitely treated as a good design for any website!

This works fine for development but in production, we need some more actions, we will briefly discuss them in the next section.

Django Deployment

Until this moment, we have discussed the development of the Django website. Now let's discuss how to move to production. Before releasing your website to production you need to check several things. First, let's go to **mybook/settings.py** and there you can find **SECRET_KEY** and **DEBUG** settings:

 # SECURITY WARNING: keep the secret key used in production secret!
SECRET_KEY = 'django-insecure-p8_-eu-rf_pf%&nttbq92r7arg1t76c*u2=$*_ge78^5-3lgid'

 # SECURITY WARNING: don't run with debug turned on in production!
DEBUG = True

DEBUG should be set to **False** in production. As for **SECRET_KEY**, it is a large random value that should be kept secret for production. It is advised to read it from an environment variable. Anyway, your production value of **SECRET_KEY** should not be added to source control!

Also, often you need to check that you have added templates and views for HTML errors (like 404). Django will display a standard page in case of an HTML error but probably this is not good enough for production.

You have got a lot of deployment options for Django: Heroku, Digital Ocean, Python Anywhere, Amazon Web Services, Microsoft Azure, etc. Feel free to choose the provider that suits your needs and budget. Most providers have the following steps for Django deployment:

- Upload the code (usually the most convenient way is to clone it from the git repository)

- Create a virtual environment and install the necessary dependencies

- Check and edit settings

- Set up the database

- Config static files. Compared to development, many more things are required for static files in production because Django doesn't handle static files automatically in production. You need to install some 3rd partly library (like WhiteNoise), then all the static files should be collected and put into a special folder (defined in settings.py) and then you need to run the command:

  >py manage.py collectstatic

After you are done, go through the website and check everything is ok and in case of errors return to the necessary point.

Chapter 5. Graphs and Data Visualization

It is really simple even for absolute beginners to draw plots using Python due to the great plotting library called Matplotlib. Matplotlib together with Numpy (another awesome Python library adding support for arrays and matrices) provides a power comparable to MATLAB which is itself a great computing platform for analyzing data. But Matplotlib is much simpler to use. Matplotlib has clear and full online documentation so I advise you to go to [5] and browse as many as possible examples there. Here we will discuss some types of graphs including pie and bar charts.

To use code samples of this chapter you need to install two Python packages - Matplotlib and Numpy:

>pip install matplotlib
>pip install numpy

Pie and Bar Charts

For pie and bar charts data we will use a small CSV file containing continents data with their area and population. Here are its first lines:

Index;Name;Population;Area
1;Asia;4,641,054,775;31,033,131
2;Africa;1,340,598,147;29,648,481

Let's start by defining our own simple **Continent** class, containing the same properties as CSV file columns - index, name, population and area:

```
class Continent:
        def __init__(self, index, name, population, area):
        self.index = index
        self.name = name
        self.population = population
        self.area = area
```

We will set the Python locale to en_US to escape problems with decimal separators which can be different for different locales (the default Python locale is taken from your system settings).

```
import locale
locale.setlocale(locale.LC_ALL, 'en_US.UTF-8')
```

As usual, let's import the necessary libraries:

```python
import matplotlib.pyplot as plt
import csv
```

And read our CSV file:

```python
with open("continents.csv", "r") as file:
    data = list(csv.reader(file, delimiter=';'))
```

Using these **data**, we can make a list of **Continent** (excluding the header, this way indexing in **data** starts from 1, not from 0):

```python
continents = [Continent(row[0], row[1], locale.atof(row[2]), locale.atof(row[3])) for row in data[1:]]
```

And just for convenience (this is not mandatory), let's make the lists of **name**, **area** and **population** properties with which we will work further:

```python
names = [c.name for c in continents]
areas = [c.area for c in continents]
populations = [c.population for c in continents]
```

Now we draw a pie chart displaying areas occupied by various continents, set its title and display it:

```python
fig, ax = plt.subplots()
ax.pie(areas, labels=names, autopct='%1.2f%%')
plt.title("Area by continent")
plt.show()
```

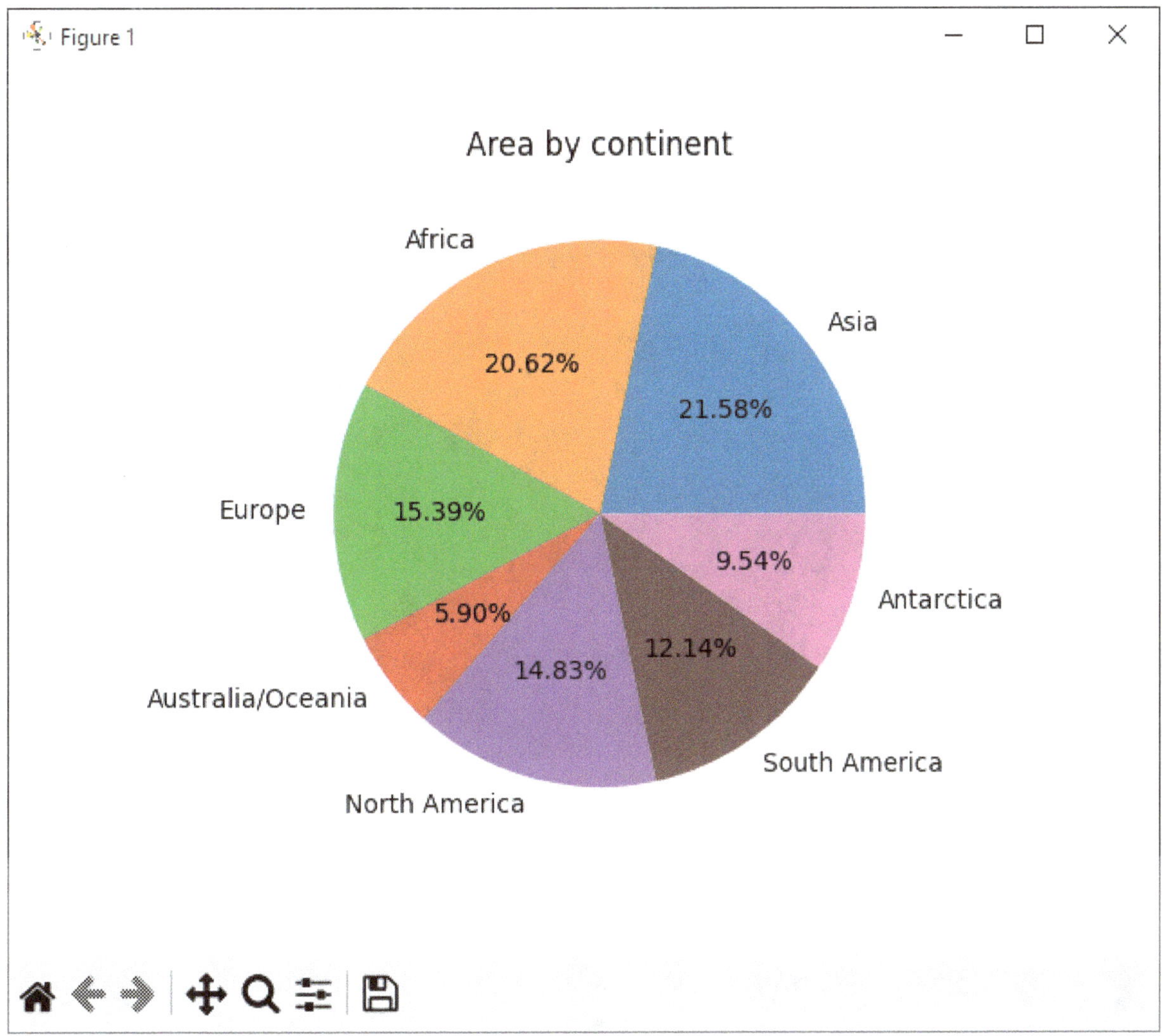

OK, so Africa is the largest continent and Australia/Oceania is the smallest.

autopct parameter is a string being used for labeling numerical values on wedges.

But what about populations? Let's draw a similar pie chart illustrating the populations of different continents. We can use the same code as in the previous sample but replace **areas** with **populations**:

```
fig, ax = plt.subplots()
ax.pie(populations, labels=names, autopct='%1.2f%%')
plt.title("Population by continent")
plt.show()
```

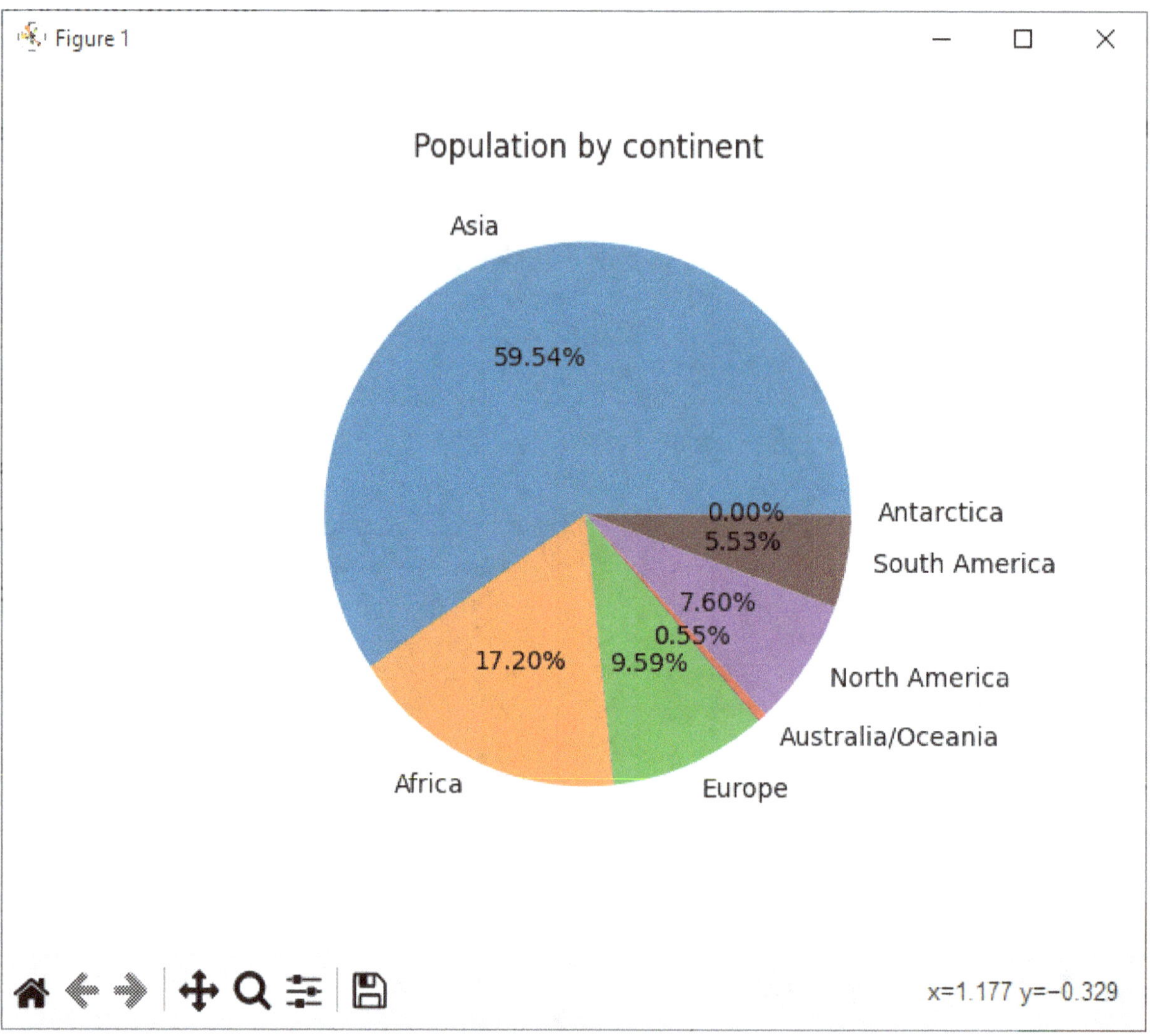

Most people live in Asia (almost 60%) and almost nobody lives in Antarctica (I guess emperor penguins were not counted).

Let's move to bar charts. They are created in the very same way, we only need to replace **ax.pie()** with **ax.bar()**. The bar charts use exactly the same data from continents.csv and we will make two similar charts, starting from areas of different continents:

```
fig, ax = plt.subplots()
ax.bar(height=areas, x=names)

ax.set_ylabel('Area')
ax.set_title('Continents by Area')

plt.show()
```

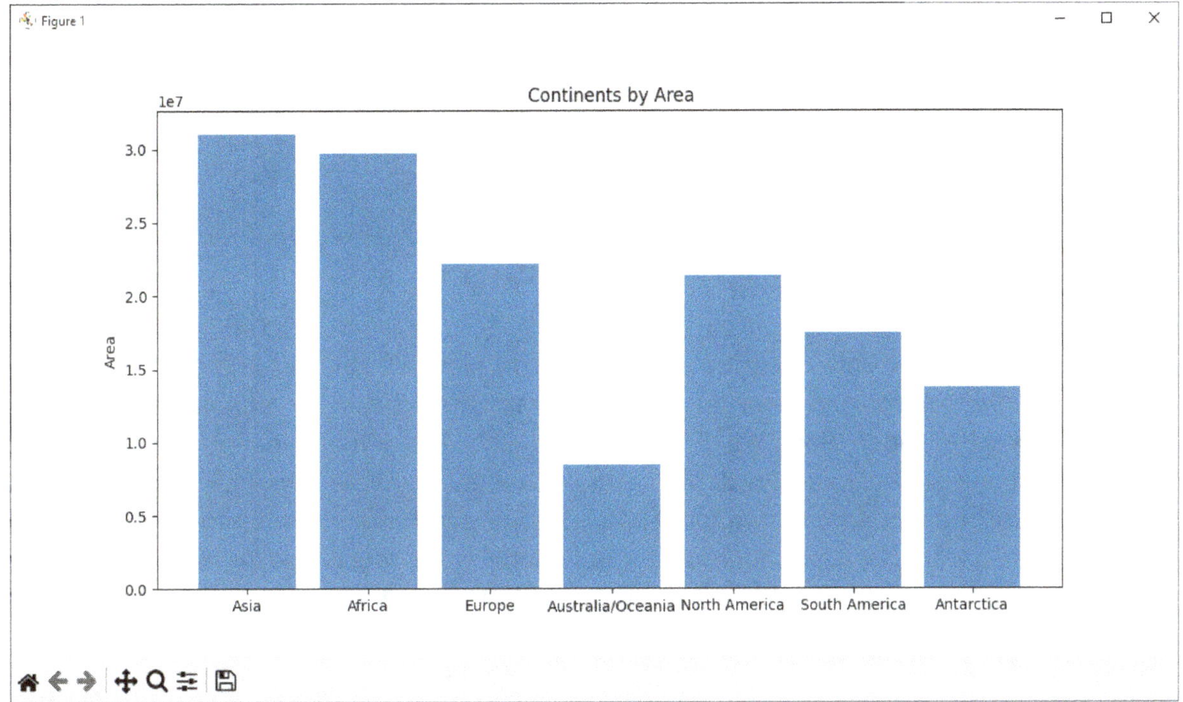

And the bar chart displaying populations:

```
fig, ax = plt.subplots()
ax.bar(height=populations, x=names, log=True)

ax.set_ylabel('Population')
ax.set_title('Continents by Population(Log scale)')

plt.show()
```

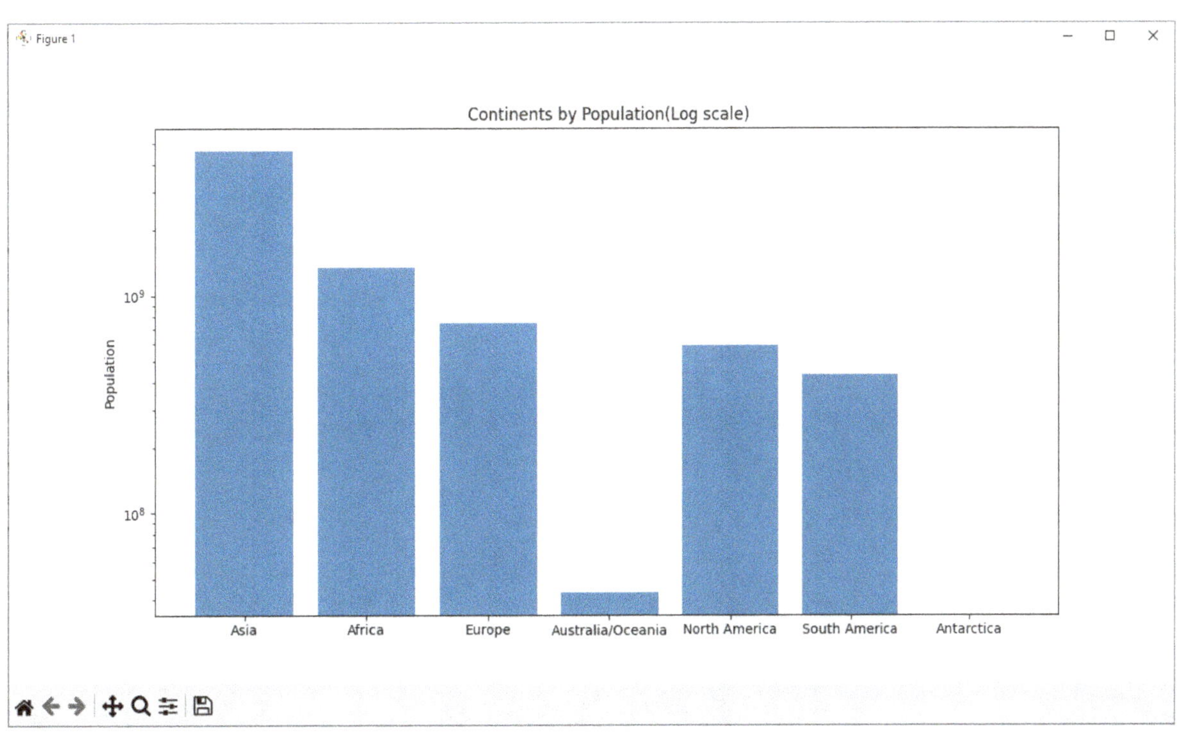

For Continents by Population it is more convenient to use a logarithmic scale because the numbers differ greatly here.

It is up to you to decide whether pie or bar charts are more appropriate for your situation.

Functions

In various situations we may need to create function plots. A function in mathematics is a rule defining the relation between one variable (called independent variable) and another variable (called dependent variable). There may be functions of many independent variables but we will consider only functions of one independent variable and call it **x**. Graphical representation of a function, i.e. a plot of this function can be very useful to understand its behavior, compare it to other functions, etc. There are special packages to work with functions and plots like MATLAB as we will see later Python tools are powerful enough for most cases.

For plotting functions we need first to import Matplotlib and Numpy:

import matplotlib.pyplot as plt
import numpy as np

We need to define **x** and **y = f(x)** coordinates for our plot. **x** is an independent variable and we can use numpy **arange()** to get the array of **x** values. We define the array of **x** as follows: start -4pi, stop 4p, step is 0.1. And for the definition of **y** we will use the Numpy **sin(x)** function.

x = np.arange(-4*np.pi,4*np.pi,0.1)
y = np.sin(x)

So we have defined our variables and we need just to tell Matplotlib to plot x and y. Also, we set the title of the graph();

plt.plot(x,y)
plt.title("The graph of sin(x)")
plt.show()

Here is what we are getting as a result:

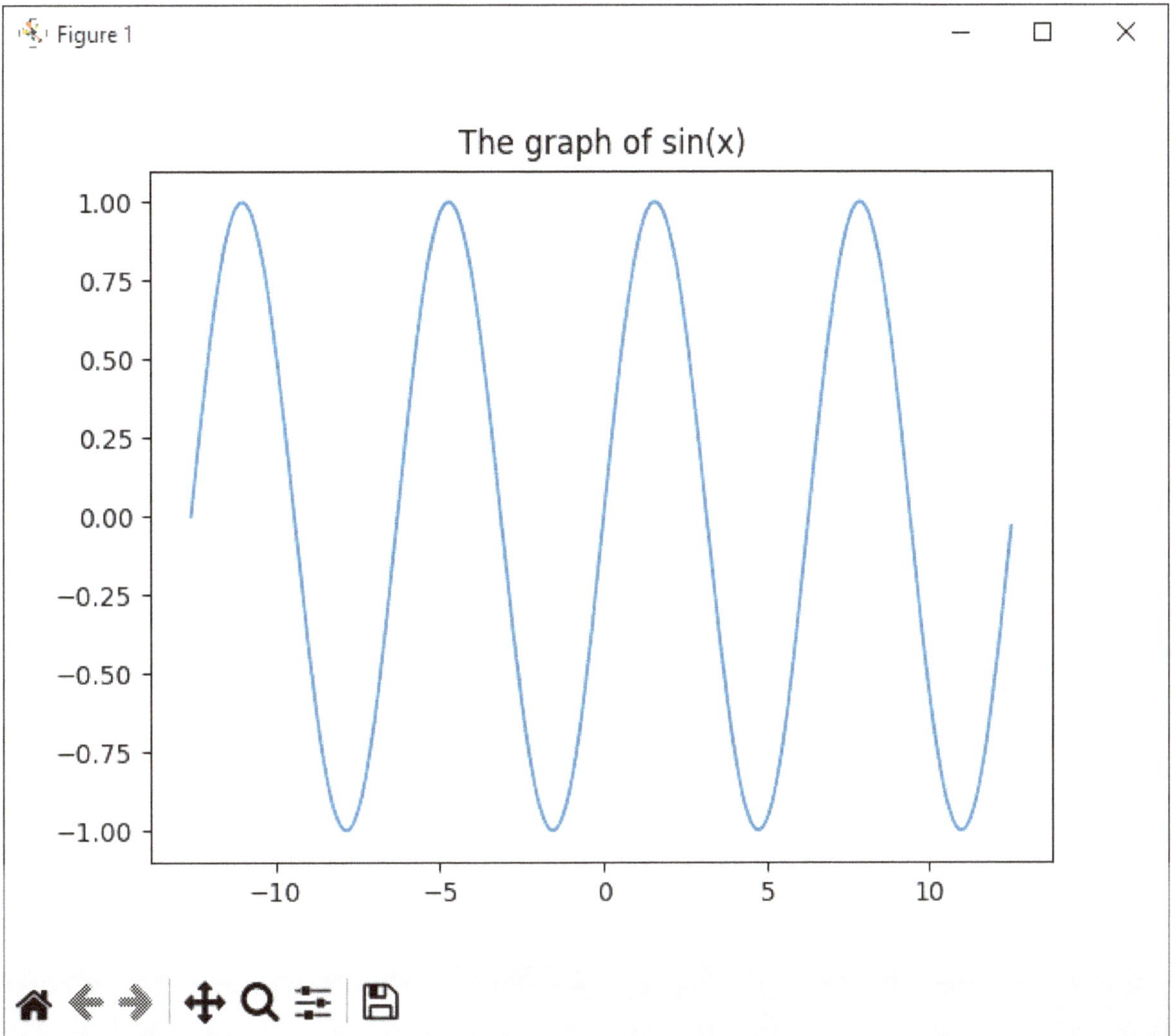

Sure, instead of **sin(x)** we can use any other function numpy supports.

In the same way we can draw several functions on one plot if you need to compare them or to look at them simultaneously. This is very convenient for function analysis.

Like in the previous sample, let's first define an array of **x** values, start is 1, stop is 10 and step is 0.1 (feel free to change these parameters while launching the code). And then we define two functions, linear and quadratic ones:

```
x = np.arange(1,10,0.1)
f1 = x
f2 = x**2
```

And let's plot given two functions, setting their color and also title and legend for the plot:

```
plt.plot(x, f1, 'r')
plt.plot(x, f2, 'g')
plt.title("The graphs of several functions")
plt.legend(['x', 'x^2'])
```

plt.show()

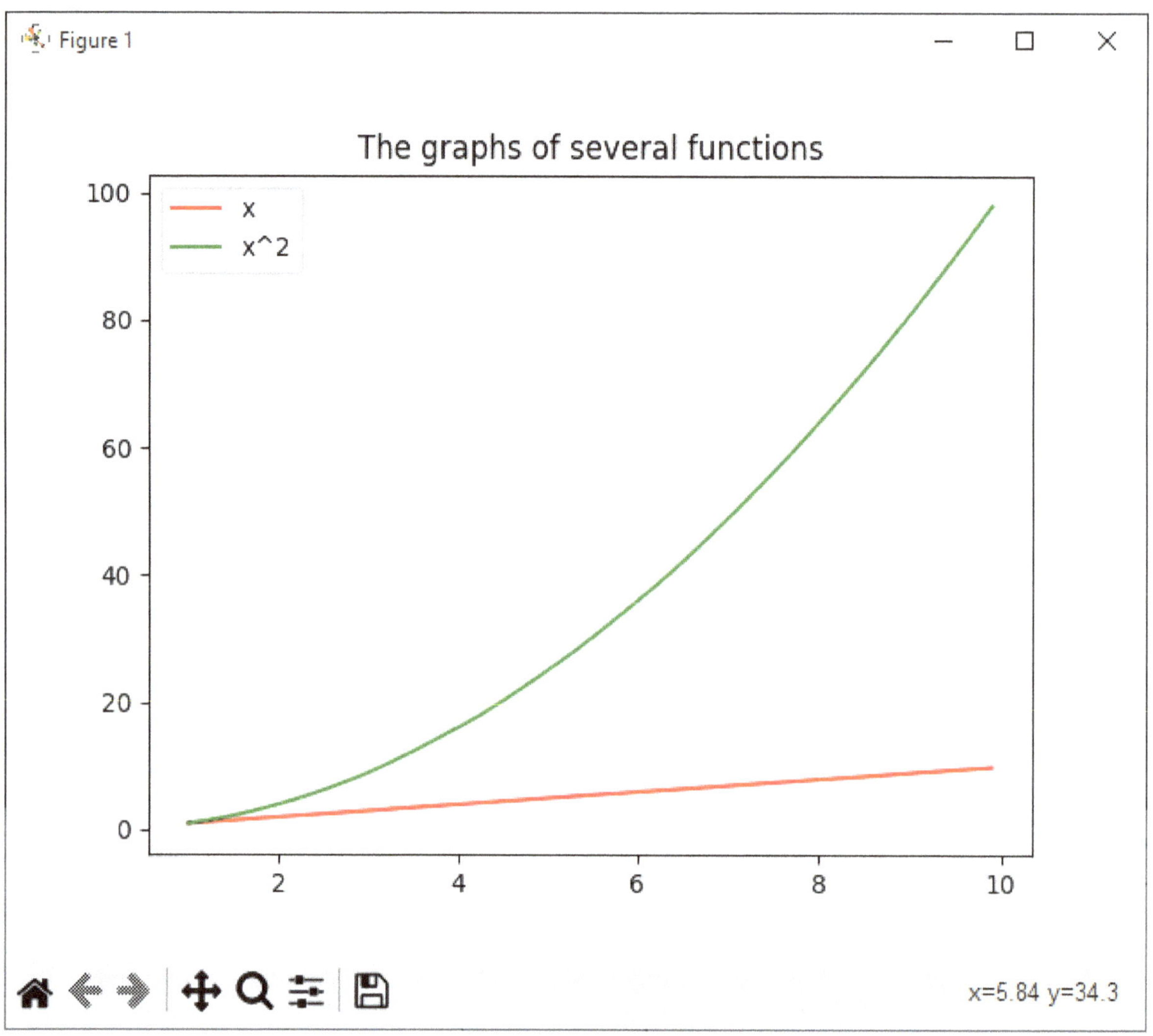

No wonder, quadratic function is growing much faster than linear. You can add another polynomial or even exponential function to this plot to check their behavior.

Plotting Experimental Data

While drawing function plots, the dependence between the variables **y** and **x** was known from the very beginning but in reality we often have another case: we have some values of **x** and values of **y** for these **x** but don't know how they are related to each other. So our aim is to draw data values and figure out something about their relationship.

Imagine we've performed an experiment with an electric circuit and measured a bunch of values for electric current and voltage respectively. Now we want to know how they are related to each other (i.e. to discover Ohm's law ourselves).

Here are the values of current (we assume it is an experimental result though they were generated by Python, see details in experiment.py in GitHub repository):

[0.958796351470367, 1.5068248405848637, 2.089912999539552, 2.46267110710l8277, 2.923919708867645, 3.4700258103702835, 4.084801907917601, 4.469183473648004, 4.983496430822813, 5.516245950586739, 6.081622558127588, 6.519373805576807, 6.936220612447363, 7.547879149280205, 7.956703620138323, 8.51634099756713, 8.998762138484722, 9.458796785879, 9.997814149984452, 10.44140301994026, 11.035762623433053, 11.523714225915942, 12.085079287811226, 12.541759852113797, 12.949414447480429, 13.551371254153045, 14.085187258426084, 14.561357200993484, 14.951773640715674, 15.459511728306943, 15.918496683900234, 16.45640383519876, 17.061338959374133, 17.585892401799097, 18.077100795435253, 18.517688284433365, 18.903139498036825, 19.54919431875562]

And the values of voltage:

[0.11409690282564222, 0.14300777050044916, 0.20154665629049012, 0.25588607388476575, 0.3100444437263696, 0.34566326705278116, 0.40756536721965564, 0.4385988715399349, 0.5118726722175914, 0.5594892773931261, 0.6113069802294879, 0.642852370199754, 0.6995120182784921, 0.7465143206789528, 0.7966940499920795, 0.8711041057446292, 0.8879197088922404, 0.9385057284830886, 1.0052445320898657, 1.0461704262382618, 1.1016817607904839, 1.155519445516234, 1.226058284203716, 1.2401093764593265, 1.312335931353926, 1.354169433461738, 1.422785902497229, 1.441763321091303, 1.4790788542293811, 1.5422708638490095, 1.594996955019707, 1.6615974798070021, 1.71133755959531, 1.74179265524484, 1.8224702435926743, 1.8561622913604525, 1.9087855433138323, 1.9737717051373416]

If you are looking at these two data arrays, it may be not easy to figure out their relationship. But if we create a plot, it will be much simpler.

Let's draw the scatter plot using these two data arrays:

```python
import matplotlib.pyplot as plt
import numpy as np

plt.xlabel('Voltage', fontsize=14)
plt.ylabel('Current', fontsize=14)
plt.plot(voltage,current,'o')
plt.title("Current vs. voltage", fontsize=20)
plt.show()
```

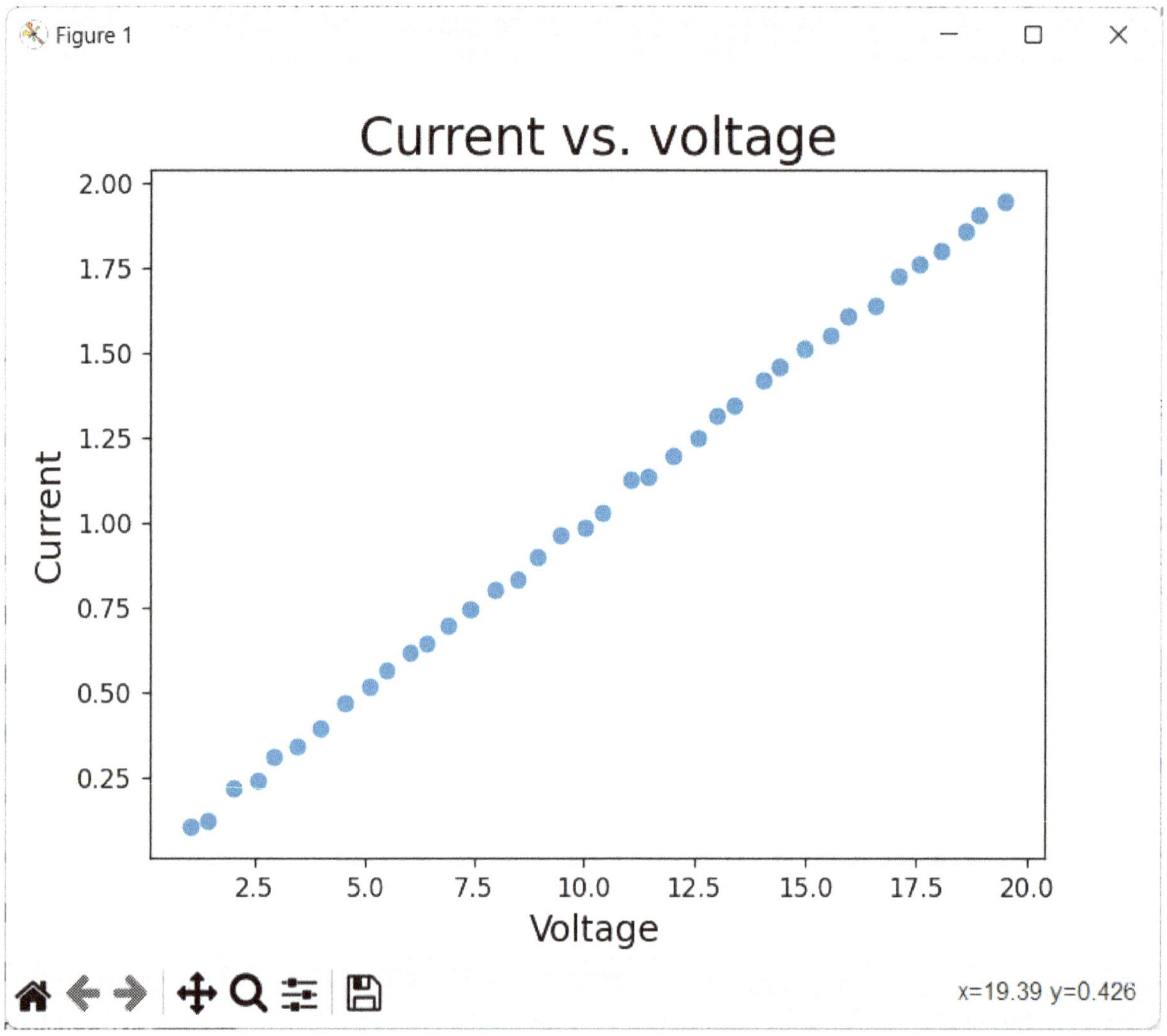

And we can approximate our dependency with linear function (this is actually Ohm's law):

```python
plt.xlabel('Voltage', fontsize=14)
plt.ylabel('Current', fontsize=14)
plt.plot(voltage,current,'o')
plt.plot(voltage, [v/10 for v in voltage], 'r')
plt.title("Current vs. voltage", fontsize=20)
plt.show()
```

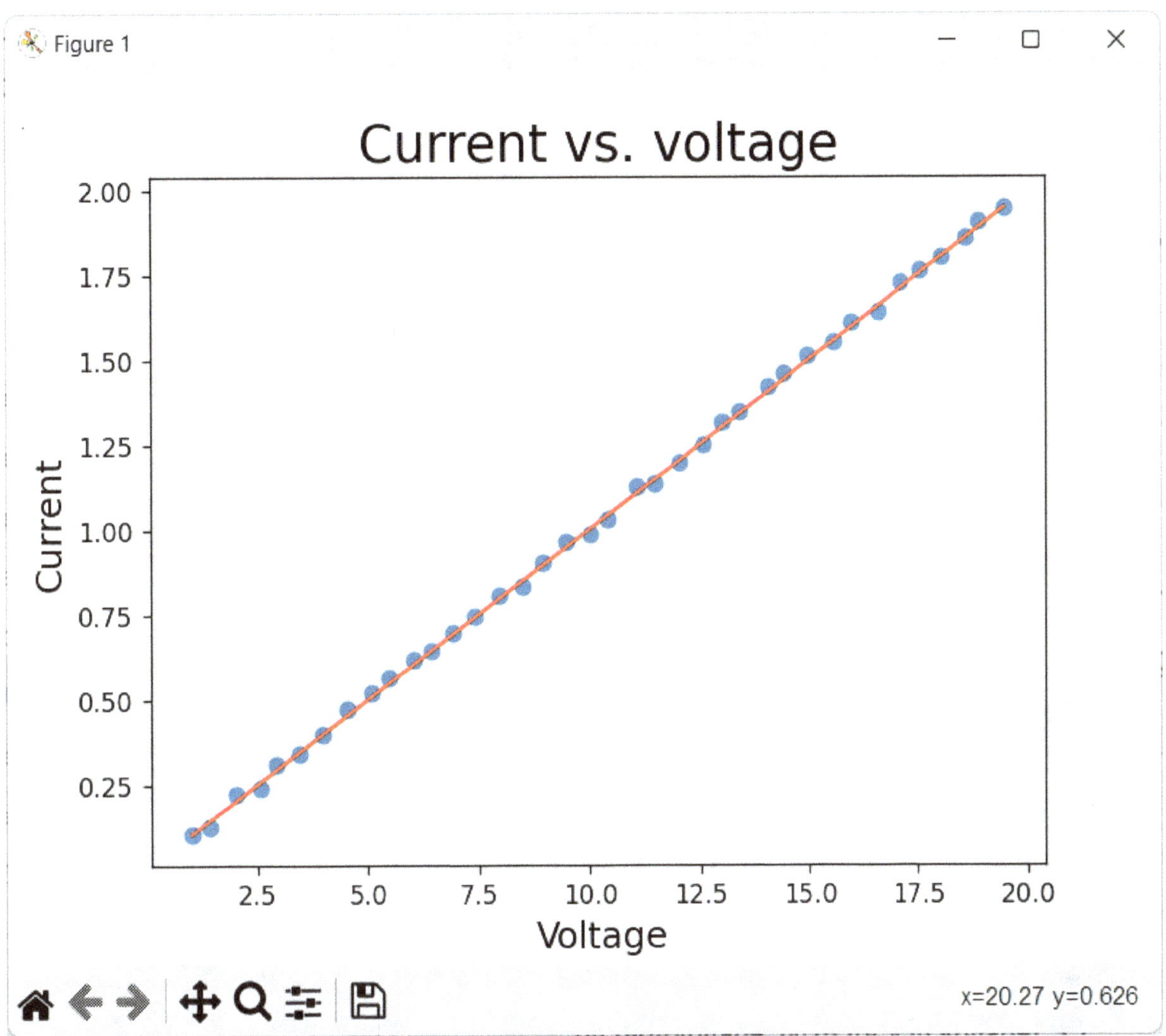

If you are interested in scientific visualizations, I advise you to read the book by Nicolas P. Rougier [7].

Chapter 6. OpenCV

OpenCV stands for Open Source Computer Vision library. It is easy to guess it mainly deals with computer vision but it has very powerful functionality having modules for image processing, video, camera, machine learning and much much more. OpenCV itself is written in C++ and it has bindings for several languages including Python.

OpenCV deserves many books devoted only to it (and they exist!) but here we won't describe its modules or classes in detail. Some mathematical operations used in this Chapter are rather complex but you should get at least an idea of how they can be used in computer vision.

Our task in this chapter will be to extract a credit card number by its photo. Here is a photo of a completely fake credit card.

First let's think about what general steps are necessary to recognize a credit card number.

1. We need to prepare our image.
2. Then we need to define the credit card number location, i.e. the location of 4 groups, each of them consisting of 4 digits(16 digits total).
3. Then we need to prepare templates (for credit card numbers a special font is usually used so we can compare our extracted pieces of image with reference images for 0-9, we will talk about it later) with which we will compare our digits and find the best match.

4. The last step is to iterate through locations from Step 2 and to recognize each digit by comparing it with a template. This means the selection of the digit which gives the best score for matching template operation.

You should already have Numpy installed (it was used in the previous chapter together with Matplotlib). This way you need to install imutils:

>pip install imutils

and OpenCV which can be tricky depending on your operating system. Try first to install pre-built CPU-only OpenCV Python package:

>pip install opencv-python

If this command doesn't work for you for some reason, try to search for instructions on installing the OpenCV Python package for your operating system.

We have finished with the libraries installation and will import headers:

```
from imutils import contours
import numpy as np
import imutils
import cv2
```

Step 1 - Image Preparation

Let's proceed with Step 1 - image preparation. The first thing we want to do is to read our fake credit card image (sure, you are welcome to use your own image or to pass input filename as program argument), resize it to a fixed width maintaining the aspect ratio and turn it to grayscale:

```
image = cv2.imread("fake-credit-card.jpeg")
image = imutils.resize(image, width=300)
gray = cv2.cvtColor(image, cv2.COLOR_BGR2GRAY)
```

We can dump our grayscale image into the file to check everything is going ok:

```
cv2.imwrite('gray.png',gray)
```

Instead of dumping to file you can use **cv2.imshow** to display the image. This can be done for all the steps.

The next part is a little more complex. We are going to perform a top-hat transform, its aim is to extract elements from the image. We create a rectangular kernel and then perform morphological top-hat transform with the specified kernel and gray image (you can think of a kernel as a matrix of small size allowing different convolution operations). This allows for revealing light regions (including numbers) against the dark background.

rectKernel = cv2.getStructuringElement(cv2.MORPH_RECT, (9, 3))
tophat = cv2.morphologyEx(gray, cv2.MORPH_TOPHAT, rectKernel)

Let's dump our image to file and have a look at it:

cv2.imwrite('tophat.png',tophat)

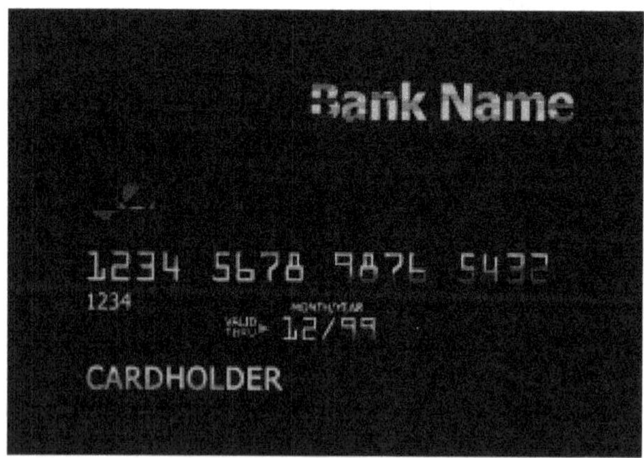

Now let's compute a Scharr gradient in X direction for the tophat image and then scale values to the range [0, 255]:

gradX = cv2.Sobel(tophat, ddepth=cv2.CV_32F, dx=1, dy=0,
**   ksize=-1)**
gradX = np.absolute(gradX)

```
(minVal, maxVal) = (np.min(gradX), np.max(gradX))
gradX = (255 * ((gradX - minVal) / (maxVal - minVal)))
gradX = gradX.astype("uint8")
```

And look at the current result:

cv2.imwrite('gradX.png',gradX)

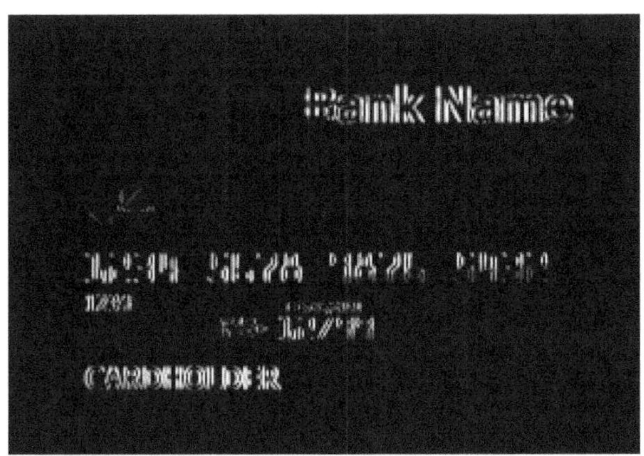

Next we need to close the gaps between digits - because we want to find the groups of digits, for this purpose we are going to use the same rectangular kernel we have used before. So we perform a closing operation and then do a binary threshold of gradX image (**THRESH_OTSU** means the threshold will be dynamically selected by the algorithm itself based on the image):

gradX = cv2.morphologyEx(gradX, cv2.MORPH_CLOSE, rectKernel)
thresh = cv2.threshold(gradX, 0, 255,
cv2.THRESH_BINARY | cv2.THRESH_OTSU)[1]

In addition to rectangular kernel let's create a square kernel 5x5 (remember to think about the kernel as a matrix which moves along the image) and make another closing operation for reducing the gaps:

squareKernel = cv2.getStructuringElement(cv2.MORPH_RECT, (5, 5))
thresh = cv2.morphologyEx(thresh, cv2.MORPH_CLOSE, squareKernel)

cv2.imwrite('thresh.png',thresh)

We can already see the areas of possible interest here, this means we finished Step 1, our image is prepared for identifying the locations of digit groups.

Step 2 - Defining Locations of Digits

Now we will pass to Step 2, defining the locations of 4 groups consisting of 4 numbers each. Let's define a function that accepts an image and returns external contours sorted from left to right - we will use it several times during this Chapter:

```python
def getContours(image):
    cntrs = cv2.findContours(image, cv2.RETR_EXTERNAL,
    cv2.CHAIN_APPROX_SIMPLE)
    cntrs =  imutils.grab_contours(cntrs)
    cntrs = contours.sort_contours(cntrs, method="left-to-right")[0]
    return cntrs
```

Let's call this function to define contours in the thresh image we've got during Step 1:

```python
cnts = getContours(thresh.copy())
```

Then we save locations of bounding rectangles of founded contours (we select only those which can match a possible group of 4 numbers - based on their aspect ratio, width and height):

```python
locs = []
```

```python
for (i, c) in enumerate(cnts):
        (x, y, w, h) = cv2.boundingRect(c)
        aspectratio = w / float(h)
        if aspectratio > 2.5 and aspectratio < 4.0:
                if (w > 40 and w < 55) and (h > 10 and h < 20):
                        locs.append((x, y, w, h))
```

locs = sorted(locs, key=lambda x:x[0])

Here **locs** should be the list with 4 values meaning the 4 groups of digits.

Step 3 - OCR-A Templates

We will use OCR-A font for template matching of the digits we found as a reference. Invented in 1966, this font is still widely used in the areas we need highly recognizable characters - both for human beings and for computers (details about OCR-1 are here [9]). This is how digits of OCR-1 font look like:

$$0123456789$$

For our reference, we will read OCR-A digits from a file, convert it to grayscale and do thresholding (i.e. converting to a binary image, with **THRESH_BINARY_INV** white areas become black and vice versa):

```
ocrA = cv2.imread("OCR-A_digits.png")
ocrA = cv2.cvtColor(ocrA, cv2.COLOR_BGR2GRAY)
ocrA = cv2.threshold(ocrA, 10, 255, cv2.THRESH_BINARY_INV)[1]
```

Then we find the contours of 10 digits using our earlier defined function **getContours()**:

```
templateCountours = getContours(ocrA.copy())
```

And get the templates for future matching, resized to the fixed size 57x88:

```
digits = {}
for (i, c) in enumerate(templateCountours):
    (x, y, w, h) = cv2.boundingRect(c)
    roi = ocrA[y:y + h, x:x + w]
    roi = cv2.resize(roi, (57, 88))
    digits[i] = roi
```

This way each digit 0 - 9 is associated with its image.

Step 4 - Matching Locations with Templates

For now we have locations for groups and, from the other side, OCR-A digit templates. Now we take the parts of the gray image for given locations, do some Gaussian blurring and thresholding and for each digit bounding rect resized to the same size 57x88 which we have used for OCR-A templates we find the best match - i.e. select the template with the maximum matching score:

```python
output = []
for (i, (gX, gY, gW, gH)) in enumerate(locs):
    groupOutput = []
    group = gray[gY - 5 : gY + gH + 5, gX - 5 : gX + gW + 5 ]
    group = cv2.GaussianBlur(group,(5,5), 0)
    group = cv2.threshold(group, 0, 255,
        cv2.THRESH_BINARY | cv2.THRESH_OTSU)[1]
    digitCountours = getContours(group.copy())

    for c in digitCountours:
        (x, y, w, h) = cv2.boundingRect(c)
        roi = group[y:y + h, x:x + w]
        roi = cv2.resize(roi, (57, 88))
        scores = []
        for (digit, digitROI) in digits.items():
            result = cv2.matchTemplate(roi, digitROI,
                cv2.TM_CCOEFF)
            (_, score, _, _) = cv2.minMaxLoc(result)
            scores.append(score)
        groupOutput.append(str(np.argmax(scores)))

    cv2.rectangle(image, (gX - 5, gY - 5), (gX + gW + 5, gY + gH + 5), (0, 0, 255), 2)
    cv2.putText(image, "".join(groupOutput), (gX, gY - 15),
cv2.FONT_HERSHEY_SIMPLEX, 0.65, (0, 0, 255), 2)

    output.extend(groupOutput)
```

For debugging purposes we also add locations and the card number text directly to the initial image.

Here is the final result with the credit card number and four group locations:

Bank Name
1234 5678 9876 5432
1234 5678 9876 5432
1234
VALID THRU
MONTH/YEAR
12/99
CARDHOLDER

Chapter 7. Machine Learning

Machine learning and deep learning are among the most popular topics related to computer science today. In this chapter we will briefly discuss machine learning and in the next chapter - deep learning. Machine learning is a very wide topic so we will concentrate only on some Python-related aspects of it.

Machine learning differs from classic algorithms in the following way: we don't tell the machine exactly what to do. Instead, we create a model based on some training data and with the help of this model try to predict the results for data the model hasn't seen during training.

Machine learning algorithms can be divided into two large groups: supervised and unsupervised. The difference between them is that supervised algorithms use labeled data for making predictions while unsupervised algorithms don't use any labeled data. The main types of supervision learning problems are classification and regression. Classification problems require a given dataset to be classified into two or more categories. Classification problems include binary classification (predicting whether a tweet has positive or negative sentiment) and multi-class classification (predicting dog breeds). In regression problems we try to get the continuous mapping function (input to output) instead. Common unsupervised learning problems include clustering (separating unlabeled data into groups) or dimensionality reduction (transforming data into a low-dimensional space reducing this way the number of features).

For our toy sample in this chapter we will split our data into train and test sets. The train set is the data you are using for your models' training, it is essential that you should never use the train set for model evaluation. This leads to overfitting and you need some independent set to say if your model is good or not. The test set allows you to estimate your models' accuracy, these are data that your model has never seen. But for more complex cases than our toy one in this chapter, it is recommended to use three sets: train set, validation set and test set. You train your models on the train set, then check your models and their hyperparameters on the validation set and finally check your model on the test set.

Iris Dataset

The first thing you need to start working in the area of machine learning or deep learning is a dataset. Preparing a dataset may be tricky and complex and we won't discuss how to prepare your own dataset correctly. For some tasks though it is possible to use existing and freely available datasets. For our samples in this chapter we will use the Iris dataset [11] which is classic and widely used for various tutorials. It is considered to be one of the earliest datasets known (dates back to R.A. Fischer, 1936). The Iris dataset contains the following columns:

- sepal length
- sepal width
- petal length

- petal width
- class

4 columns (widths and heights) are continuous features and class is what we should predict. There are 3 classes each with 50 samples in this dataset.

The main reason for using Python for machine and deep learning tasks is its great machine learning libraries. In the scope of this chapter we will use scikit-learn, a free software machine learning library for Python and in the next chapter we will move on to a few deep learning libraries. scikit-learn allows us to solve successfully both supervised (classification, regression) and unsupervised (clustering, dimensionality reduction) problems.

Let's proceed with scikit-learn installation:

>pip install -U scikit-learn

Also, in addition to Matplotlib and Numpy we've used already in previous chapters we will need to install pandas and seaborn libraries:

> pip install pandas
> pip install seaborn

Pandas is a data processing and CSV files input/output library. Seaborn is a Python graphing library.

Let's start as usual with the import of libraries:

```
import pandas as pd
import numpy as np
import seaborn as sns
import matplotlib.pyplot as plt

from sklearn import tree
from sklearn.metrics import accuracy_score, classification_report
from sklearn.datasets import load_iris
from sklearn.tree import DecisionTreeClassifier
from sklearn.cluster import KMeans
from sklearn.model_selection import train_test_split

import warnings
warnings.filterwarnings('ignore')
```

The last part is added to ignore the warnings because seaborn often generates a bunch of warnings that we don't need.

Next we load the Iris dataset (seaborn actually loads the dataset from the online repository so an internet connection is required here):

```python
iris = sns.load_dataset('iris')
```

and print its head (first rows of the dataset):

```
   sepal_length  sepal_width  petal_length  petal_width species
0           5.1          3.5           1.4          0.2  setosa
1           4.9          3.0           1.4          0.2  setosa
2           4.7          3.2           1.3          0.2  setosa
3           4.6          3.1           1.5          0.2  setosa
4           5.0          3.6           1.4          0.2  setosa
```

Note that seaborn is strongly integrated with pandas and **load_dataset()** function returns **pandas.Dataframe**.

We can print information about dataset using

```python
print(iris.info())
```

It returns the following:

```
<class 'pandas.core.frame.DataFrame'>
RangeIndex: 150 entries, 0 to 149
Data columns (total 5 columns):
 #   Column        Non-Null Count  Dtype
---  ------        --------------  -----
 0   sepal_length  150 non-null    float64
 1   sepal_width   150 non-null    float64
 2   petal_length  150 non-null    float64
 3   petal_width   150 non-null    float64
 4   species       150 non-null    object
dtypes: float64(4), object(1)
memory usage: 6.0+ KB
```

There are no missing values in the dataset, it consists of 5 columns and 150 rows.

Exploratory Data Analysis

Seaborn graphs allow us to analyze easily for the Iris dataset how the output depends on each of the 4 features.

```python
fig, axes = plt.subplots(2, 2)

ax = sns.boxplot(x="species", y="sepal_length", data=iris, orient='v',
    ax=axes[0, 0])
ax = sns.boxplot(x="species", y="sepal_width", data=iris, orient='v',
    ax=axes[0, 1])
ax = sns.boxplot(x="species", y="petal_length", data=iris, orient='v',
```

```python
    ax=axes[1, 0])
ax = sns.boxplot(x="species", y="petal_width", data=iris, orient='v',
    ax=axes[1, 1])

plt.show()
```

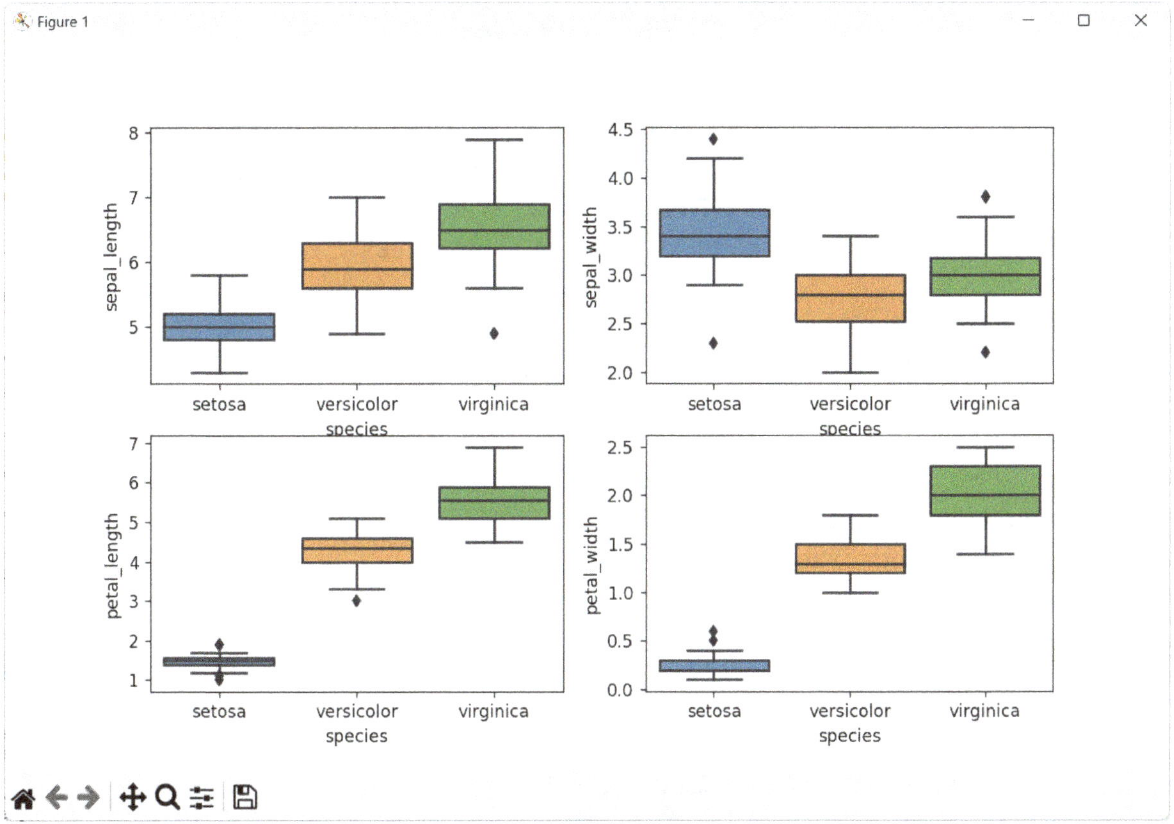

It is clear that **petal_length** and **petal_width** allow us to define species (their values are different for each result) so these two features are more important for us. This step is known as EDA (Exploratory Data Analysis) - analysis and visualization of your dataset.

EDA may be really important for future model building. It may turn out that features have a very different scale then you need to apply proper scaling as the next step. If there are a lot of features, it is wise to select only important ones. In our simple case these things are not necessary.

Now let's make a couple of models for the Iris dataset. We will try both supervised and unsupervised approaches. For model training and prediction we will split the Iris dataset into training and test sets:

```python
X = iris.iloc[:, :-1]
y = iris.iloc[:, -1]


X_train, X_test, y_train, y_test = train_test_split(X, y,
                    test_size=0.3,
                    random_state = 105)
```

So we have 70% of the data in the training set and 30% of the data in the test set. **random_state** can be any integer value, it is not necessary to pass it but passing it explicitly allows reproducing the same results.

Decision Trees

First we will try to use Decision Trees (DT). DT is a simple non-parametric supervised machine learning method and it can be used both for classification and regression problems. scikit-learn provides **DecisionTreeClassifier**, a class for doing multi-class classification for datasets. So we create a **DecisionTreeClassifier** object and then fit our train set. During this step DT tries to create decision rules based on data features.

```
dt = DecisionTreeClassifier()
dt.fit(X_train, y_train)
```

To get an idea of what is going inside, we can plot the decision tree:

```
plt.figure(figsize=(15, 10))
tree.plot_tree(dt, filled=True)
plt.show()
```

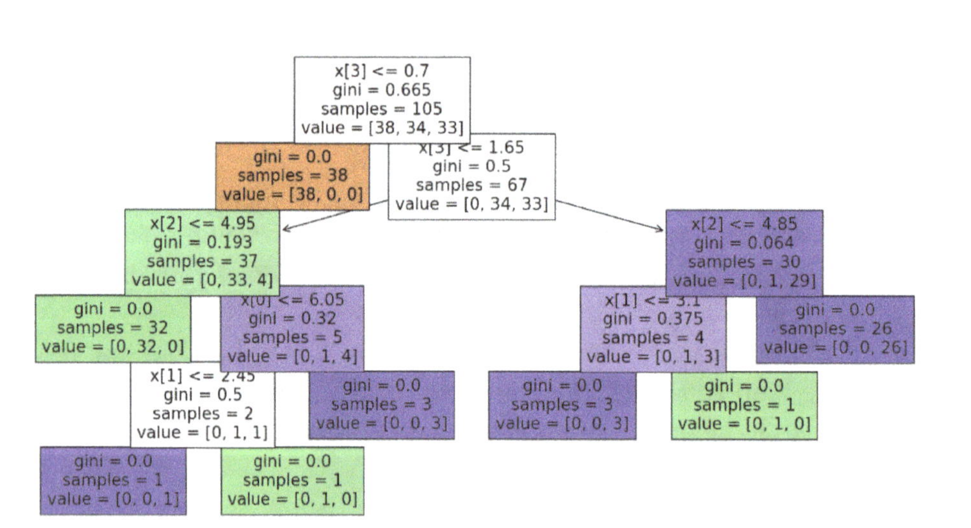

Here we can check what decisions were being made. The initial decision is based on x[3] column - petal_length which seems to be reasonable according to EDA.

Now we can predict the values for the test set:

```
y_pred = dt.predict(X_test)
```

And compare them with known values:

```
print(accuracy_score(y_pred, y_test))
print(classification_report(y_pred, y_test))
```

0.9777777777777777

```
              precision    recall  f1-score   support

      setosa       1.00      1.00      1.00        12
  versicolor       0.94      1.00      0.97        15
   virginica       1.00      0.94      0.97        18

    accuracy                           0.98        45
   macro avg       0.98      0.98      0.98        45
weighted avg       0.98      0.98      0.98        45
```

So accuracy of DT on this train/test split is about 98% percent - a quite good result for such a simple method.

The advantages of DT are its simplicity and the fact that you can understand what is really going on with the help of decision tree plotting. The main drawback is possible overfitting (often it doesn't generalize well). Also DT is often unstable, adding a small new portion of data can change the decision tree dramatically.

K-Means Clustering

K-Means is an unsupervised machine learning algorithm that is used for clustering problems. Basically, it works as follows:

- we select parameter K, which is a number of clusters. For the Iris dataset, it is reasonable to select K=3. If your selected number of clusters is definitely wrong, you won't receive any reasonable output, in this case you may try another value of parameter K.
- we choose random centers for each cluster, they are called centroids. For K=3, we will have 3 centroids.
- we assign each point in the dataset to its closest centroid.
- we recalculate centroids as average for all points belonging to its cluster.
- we iteratively repeat the previous two steps until the maximum number of iterations is reached or centroids do not change anymore.

Let's look at how it is done in practice with the Iris dataset. First, initialize KMeans with K=3 and fit our train set:

```
kmeans = KMeans(n_clusters=3, random_state=42)
```

kmeans.fit(X_train)

Then predict values on the test set:

y_pred = kmeans.predict(X_test)

Finally we need to estimate the model accuracy by comparing the predicted values with the given output (encoding species output as 0,1,2):

y_test.replace({'setosa': 0, 'versicolor':2, 'virginica':1}, inplace=True)

print(classification_report(y_test, y_pred))

```
              precision    recall  f1-score   support

           0       1.00      1.00      1.00        12
           1       0.93      0.76      0.84        17
           2       0.79      0.94      0.86        16

    accuracy                           0.89        45
   macro avg       0.91      0.90      0.90        45
weighted avg       0.90      0.89      0.89        45
```

So the accuracy of K-Means clustering is about 90% (remember it depends on random values so it can vary). Anyway, with a good choice of K this method can give an acceptable result.

Chapter 8. Deep Learning

Deep learning is a kind of machine learning which we discussed in Chapter 7. The word "deep" means that model architecture has multiple layers (including an input layer, several hidden layers and an output layer). If a network has only one hidden layer, it is often called shallow.

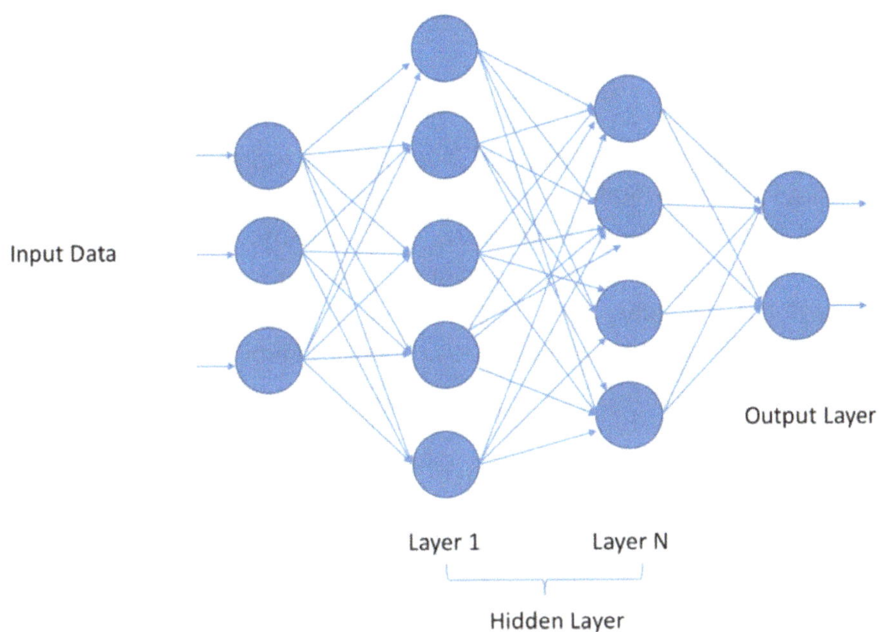

There is a theoretical result that states that even one hidden layer with a lot of neurons and a non-linear activation is enough to fit any function. But in practice, it is better to add many hidden layers because you can easily add more parameters to your model this way. Therefore having more parameters in the model allows for fitting complex functions. However, adding too much hidden layers can lead to overfitting - when your model behaves great on the training set but poorly on the test set (unseen data). Having a lot of layers allows the model just to memorize all the train set features but prevents good generalization. We will discuss how to conquer it later in this Chapter.

Typical architectures for deep learning include multi-layer perceptrons (MLP) - we have just briefly described them, convolutional neural networks (CNN) - they are especially good for image input - and recurrent neural networks (RNN) - they are often used for natural language processing.

Convolutional neural networks

We are going to work with images so we will focus on CNN in this Chapter. Here is a general scheme of CNN:

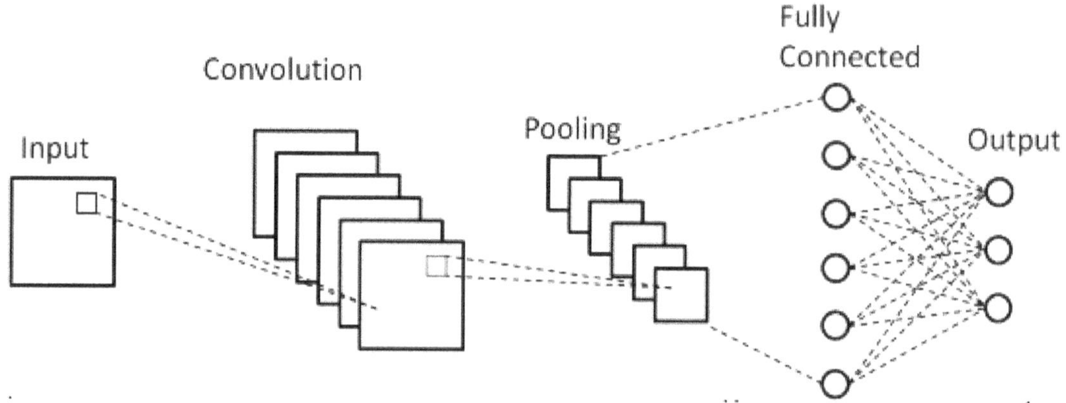

CNN has an input layer, hidden layers and an output layer but it is more specific about what its hidden layers are. They are convolutional layers, pooling layers and fully connected layers. In each convolution layer we take a small-size kernel and move it along the image (we had a similar operation in Chapter 6). Performing convolution operations allows for finding different image features. Usually, the earliest layers find simple features and the latest ones find more complicated and specific features. These convolutional layers are the heart of CNN.

Pooling layers are used for downsampling the image, which allows to reduce the number of parameters and avoids overfitting. Pooling layers are really simple, usually max pooling is used which means just a maximum value is selected. Between convolution and pooling layers, often activation layers are inserted to add non-linearity to the model.

After passing convolutional and pooling labels the input is fed into fully connected layers and then to the output layer.

One of the reasons why CNNs recently have become so popular and efficient is that it is now possible to train them on GPUs. GPUs (that is Graphics Processing Unit) initially designed for processing high-resolution images and graphics is generally much better for training deep neural networks (including CNN) compared to CPUs (stands for Central Processing Unit). GPUs can better use parallel processing - dividing smaller tasks between their multiple cores. For deep learning with its large datasets this is extremely important and efficient. Running a lot of tasks in parallel with GPUs allows for much faster training.

If you are going to work with images and deep learning, you should know about ImageNet. It is a very large visual database consisting currently more than 14 million images. The aim of ImageNet is to provide 1000 images on average per "synonym set" (it is the name for some meaningful concept, a word, multiple words, or a phrase). Moreover, ImageNet is a research team, a community, and a project. Each year they hold an ImageNet contest and different kinds of CNN usually win in it so we can track progress in this area. For example, in 2017, 29 of 38 competing teams had greater than 95% accuracy.

CNNs have their own evolution, for example, let's compare one of the earliest CNNs - LeNet proposed by LeCun et al. in 1998, and AlexNet, the first CNN that won the ImageNet competition in 2012. Here is the comparison of LeNet and AlexNet taken from [12].

LeNet	**AlexNet**
Image: 28 (height) × 28 (width) × 1 (channel)	Image: 224 (height) × 224 (width) × 3 (channels)
Convolution with 5×5 kernel+2 padding: 28×28×6	Convolution with 11×11 kernel+4 stride: 54×54×96
↓ sigmoid	↓ ReLu
Pool with 2×2 average kernel+2 stride: 14×14×6	Pool with 3×3 max. kernel+2 stride: 26×26×96
Convolution with 5×5 kernel (no pad): 10×10×16	Convolution with 5×5 kernel+2 pad: 26×26×256
↓ sigmoid	↓ ReLu
Pool with 2×2 average kernel+2 stride: 5×5×16	Pool with 3×3 max. kernel+2 stride: 12×12×256
↓ flatten	
Dense: 120 fully connected neurons	Convolution with 3×3 kernel+1 pad: 12×12×384
↓ sigmoid	↓ ReLu
Dense: 84 fully connected neurons	Convolution with 3×3 kernel+1 pad: 12×12×384
↓ sigmoid	↓ ReLu
Dense: 10 fully connected neurons	Convolution with 3×3 kernel+1 pad: 12×12×256
	↓ ReLu
Output: 1 of 10 classes	Pool with 3×3 max. kernel+2 stride: 5×5×256
	↓ flatten
	Dense: 4096 fully connected neurons
	↓ ReLu, dropout p=0.5
	Dense: 4096 fully connected neurons
	↓ ReLu, dropout p=0.5
	Dense: 1000 fully connected neurons
	Output: 1 of 1000 classes

You can see that AlexNet is much more complex (more layers, different kernels, etc.)

In this Chapter, we will use Residual Neural Networks (ResNet). It is a very popular classifier architecture (depending on the layer number, it can be ResNet18, ResNet34, ResNet50, ResNet151, and others). ResNet tries to address the following problem: just adding more and more layers is not always better because the layers repeat themselves and the features they are trying to learn. The authors of ResNet suggested an "identity shortcut connection" that skips one or more layers. The skip connections solve the problem of vanishing gradient for deep learning in many cases that's why ResNets are really successful for many image classification problems.

Deep Learning Python Libraries

Creating a CNN from scratch is not going to be easy. The real Python power for deep learning tasks is having the greatest libraries ever. Let's briefly cover some of these libraries. We won't get into the details of installation, just go through various libraries and show pieces of pseudocode illustrating how you can create a CNN using them.

TensorFlow (see [13]) is a free and open-source library initially developed by the Google Brain for internal Google use. In 2019 Tensorflow 2.0 version was released. Tensorflow supports a huge number of platforms - from mobile devices to powerful server clusters. Also, it supports CPUs, GPUs, and TPUs (stands for Tensor Processing Unit). TPU is an application-specific integrated circuit (ASIC) built by Google specially for machine learning and for using Tensorflow.

TensorFlow API uses Keras to allow users to make their own machine learning models. Keras is an open-source library providing a Python interface to various backends. Its main backend is Tensorflow and in different versions, it supports also Theano, PlaidML, PyTorch and others. The aim of Keras is to enable fast prototyping and reduce the amount of required code. Defining the model in Keras involves adding the layers we have already seen (convolutional, pooling, softmax):

```
from tensorflow.keras.models import Sequential
from tensorflow.keras.layers import Conv2D, MaxPooling2D, Dense, Flatten

num_filters = 8
filter_size = 3
pool_size = 2

# Build the model.
model = Sequential([
  Conv2D(num_filters, filter_size, input_shape=(28, 28, 1)),
  MaxPooling2D(pool_size=pool_size),
  Flatten(),
  Dense(10, activation='softmax'),
])
```

Another, more advanced option is to define your model as a class. Anyway, after the model is ready, we can load or save its weights, fit the model using the training set and then predict values for the test set.

An alternative to Tensorflow/Keras is PyTorch [14]. It is an open-source Python package providing GPU accelerated tensors computation and deep neural networks implementation. Using PyTorch at first maybe a little more difficult compared to Keras. To build your own model in PyTorch you need to create your own class extending **nn.Module** from PyTorch which already provides a bunch of useful methods:

```
class ConvNeuralNet(nn.Module):
  def __init__(self, num_classes):
    super(ConvNeuralNet, self).__init__()
    self.conv_layer1 = nn.Conv2d(in_channels=3, out_channels=32, kernel_size=3)
    self.conv_layer2 = nn.Conv2d(in_channels=32, out_channels=32, kernel_size=3)
    self.max_pool1 = nn.MaxPool2d(kernel_size = 2, stride = 2)

    self.conv_layer3 = nn.Conv2d(in_channels=32, out_channels=64, kernel_size=3)
    self.conv_layer4 = nn.Conv2d(in_channels=64, out_channels=64, kernel_size=3)
    self.max_pool2 = nn.MaxPool2d(kernel_size = 2, stride = 2)
```

```python
        self.fc1 = nn.Linear(1600, 128)
        self.relu1 = nn.ReLU()
        self.fc2 = nn.Linear(128, num_classes)

    def forward(self, x):
        out = self.conv_layer1(x)
        out = self.conv_layer2(out)
        out = self.max_pool1(out)

        out = self.conv_layer3(out)
        out = self.conv_layer4(out)
        out = self.max_pool2(out)

        out = out.reshape(out.size(0), -1)

        out = self.fc1(out)
        out = self.relu1(out)
        out = self.fc2(out)
        return out
```

As you can see, in __init__ we define the layers of the CNN (convolutional, pooling, fully connected). Another necessary function is **forward()** where you define the forward pass, i.e. how the input data goes through the network.

Let's talk about one more great Python library - fastai - see [15] for reference. fastai is a deep learning library that provides high-level components for its users so we won't need to create every minor detail (though it is still necessary to understand what is going on behind the code - that is very important for any deep learning library). fastai is based on PyTorch and compatible with it so you can have one part of your project written using plain PyTorch and another part written using fastai. It allows us to reach very good results really quickly. Let's look at the CNN example using fastai:

```python
from fastai.vision.all import *

dls = ImageDataLoaders.from_name_func(path, files, label_func,
item_tfms=Resize(224))

learn = vision_learner(dls, resnet34, metrics=error_rate) learn.fine_tune(1)
learn.predict(new_image)
```

So first we do the import of stuff related to computer vision in fastai. Then, in the second line, we feed the training data (image files) into the model. We create a Learner fastai object combining the data and model for training - we have specified ResNet34 CNN architecture. And that's it! What's left - we just fine-tune the model (for just one epoch in this piece of code) and do the prediction for the new image. That is easy - so let's try to do our own example with fastai and cover it in more detail.

CIFAR-10 Classification with fastai

Our example will cover image classification of the CIFAR-10 dataset [16] using fastai. The CIFAR-10 dataset consists of 60,000 small color images (their size is 32x32). Each of these images corresponds to one of 10 classes (airplane, automobile, bird, cat, deer, dog, frog, horse, ship, truck). 60,000 images can be split into 50,000 train set and 10,000 test set. This dataset is a labeled subset of 80 million tiny images dataset collected by Alex Krizhevsky, Vinod Nair, and Geoffrey Hinton.

Our aim is to perform image classification of the CIFAR-10 dataset with fastai and estimate the accuracy of the results. Human accuracy is estimated as 94% (which means the error rate is about 6%) for this dataset. The accuracy of the best CNNs nowadays is about 99% (so their error rate is about 1% or even less).

We are going to use Google Colab [17] for running our code. Google Colab is a great and easy-to-use tool that helps you to skip setting up your own environment (this step may be complex for deep learning tasks) and moreover, gives you free access to GPU. Using Google Colab you can create a new Jupiter Notebook (this is a file with .ipynb extension, this stands for Interactive Python Notebook) and run it (separate cells or all the notebook). Jupiter Notebook itself is a web-based environment that allows you to combine text, code, visualizations, etc.

Another option you can try to get access to Jupiter notebooks and GPU is a Kaggle kernel - Kaggle provides more powerful GPUs so training there should be faster. It requires only registration on https://www.kaggle.com. All the Google Colab code is the same for Kaggle.

First of all, let's check that fastai is installed in the Google Colab sheet and if not, install it with its dependencies:

!pip install fastai

And import necessary for computer vision part of fastai headers:

from fastai.vision.all import *

Sure, we need the dataset itself so we download it by the given URL:

path = untar_data(URLs.CIFAR)

Then we create data loader template and dataloaders:

```
data = DataBlock(blocks=(ImageBlock(), CategoryBlock()),
        get_items=get_image_files,
        get_y=parent_label,
        item_tfms=Resize(40))

dataloader = data.dataloaders(path, bs=64, valid_pct=0.2, seed=42,)
```

bs is the number of samples per batch, in our case 64. We split randomly our data to train and validation set and set the size of the validation set to 20% (**valid_pct=0.2**).

Just to make sure everything goes fine, let's show some of the images:

dataloader.valid.show_batch(max_n=12, nrows=3)

Now let's use **vision_learner()** function to create a **Learner** object with pretrained ResNet34 model. **Learner** handles training in fastai and manages model as well as loss function.

learner34 = vision_learner(dataloader, resnet34, metrics=accuracy)

Then tune our **Learner** for the given number of epochs, in our code it is 10:

learner34.fine_tune(10)

It prints the results for each epoch so we can track train loss, validation loss and accuracy:

epoch	train_loss	valid_loss	accuracy	time
0	0.751568	0.634223	0.781333	28:09
1	0.578851	0.537214	0.816083	28:20
2	0.456947	0.497603	0.833500	29:12
3	0.336738	0.483010	0.844250	28:36
4	0.207417	0.512145	0.848917	28:57
5	0.118600	0.568659	0.854667	29:02
6	0.060828	0.617221	0.857250	28:26
7	0.024544	0.678964	0.859417	27:28
8	0.012252	0.693337	0.863083	27:15
9	0.006851	0.699739	0.863667	26:46

We have reached 86% accuracy, this is a good result for such a simple code. Train loss is decreasing nearly to 0 during 10 epochs. Validation loss decreases for a few epochs but then starts to increase which is probably a sign of overfitting (the model has adjusted to train set too well and does worse in general). Can we do better? Yes, we can reduce the number of epochs and try something different.

Let's finish our first run by looking at the confusion matrix:

```
interp34 = ClassificationInterpretation.from_learner(learner34)
interp34.plot_confusion_matrix(figsize=(13,10))
```

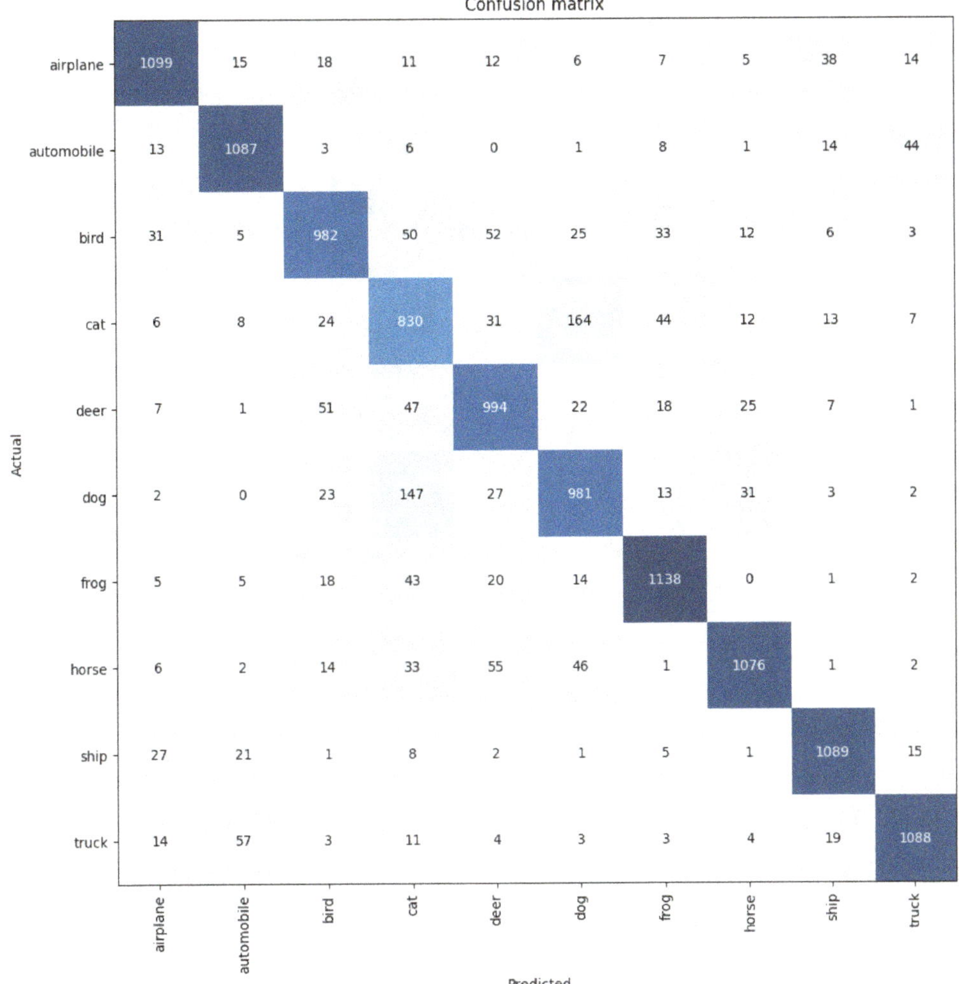

And plotting the top losses:

interp34.plot_top_losses(12, nrows=4, figsize=(13, 8))

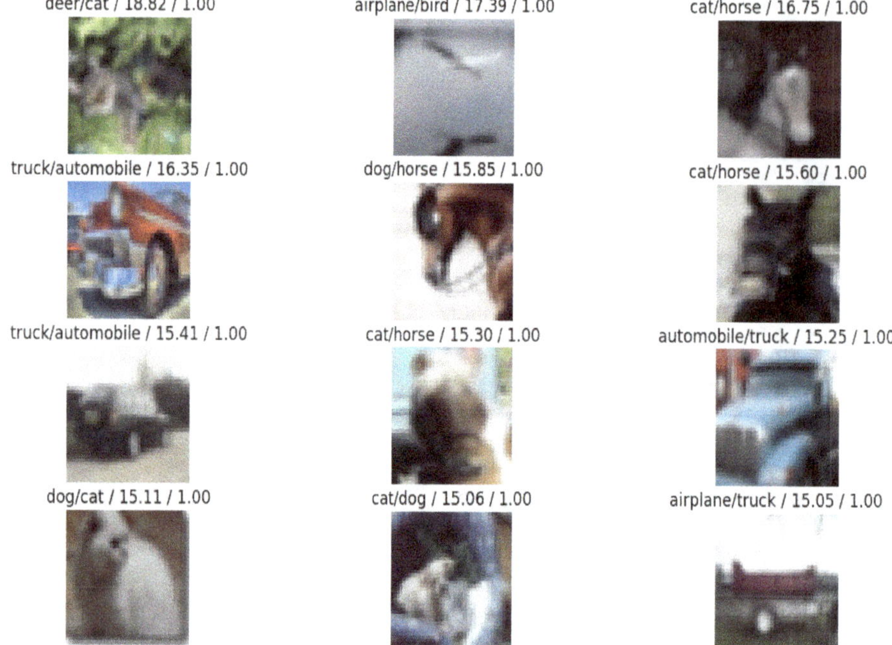

Great, now let's try to implement our idea regarding reducing epochs number and trying something better or different. After importing and downloading data let's modify our code with dataloaders:

```
data = DataBlock(blocks=(ImageBlock(), CategoryBlock()),
        get_items=get_image_files,
        get_y=parent_label,
        item_tfms=Resize(224))

dataloader = data.dataloaders(path, bs=64, valid_pct=0.2, seed=42,)
```

And check the images:

```
dataloader.valid.show_batch(max_n=12, nrows=3)
```

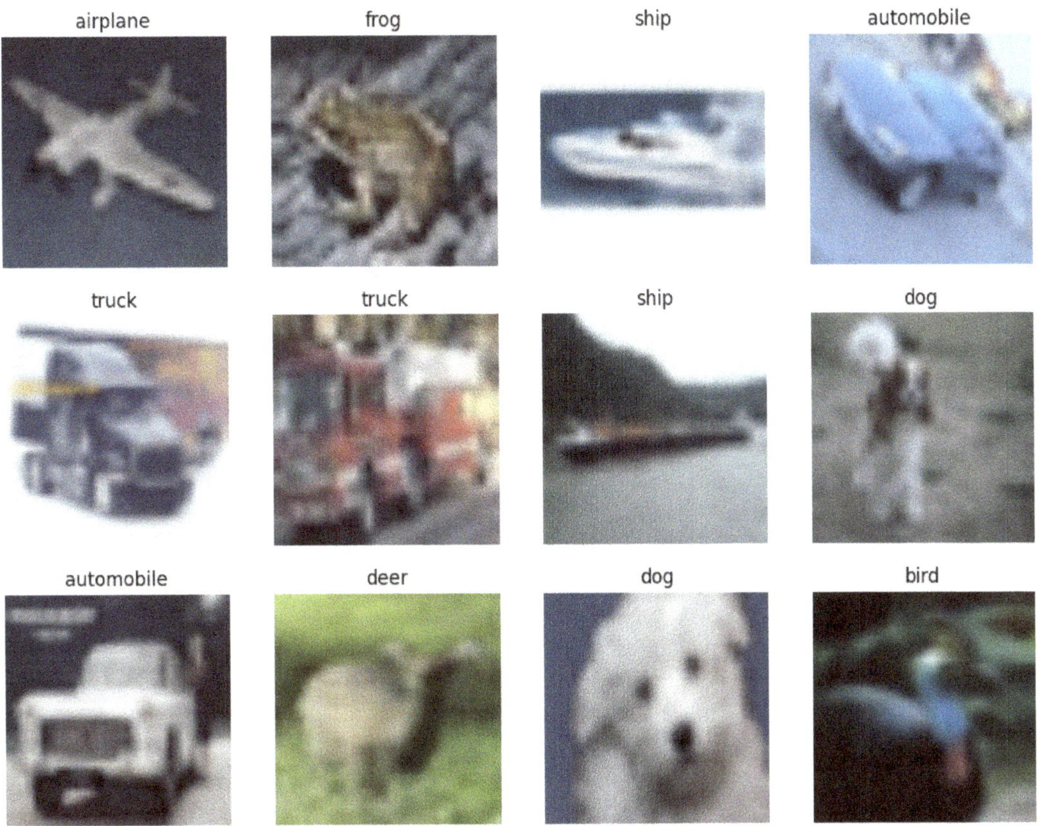

Note we resize our small images to a larger size, 224x224. It is a size that the ResNet34 network was trained on so the results should be better. Let's create a Learner object as we did before:

learner34 = vision_learner(dataloader, resnet34, metrics=accuracy)

Instead of training start, let's first detect the good learning rate (this is a hyperparameter that shows how much your model changes in response to losses). Learning rate is important because if it is too small, your model doesn't learn quickly and if it is too large, the model becomes unstable. So we need an optimal learning rate:

learner34.lr_find()

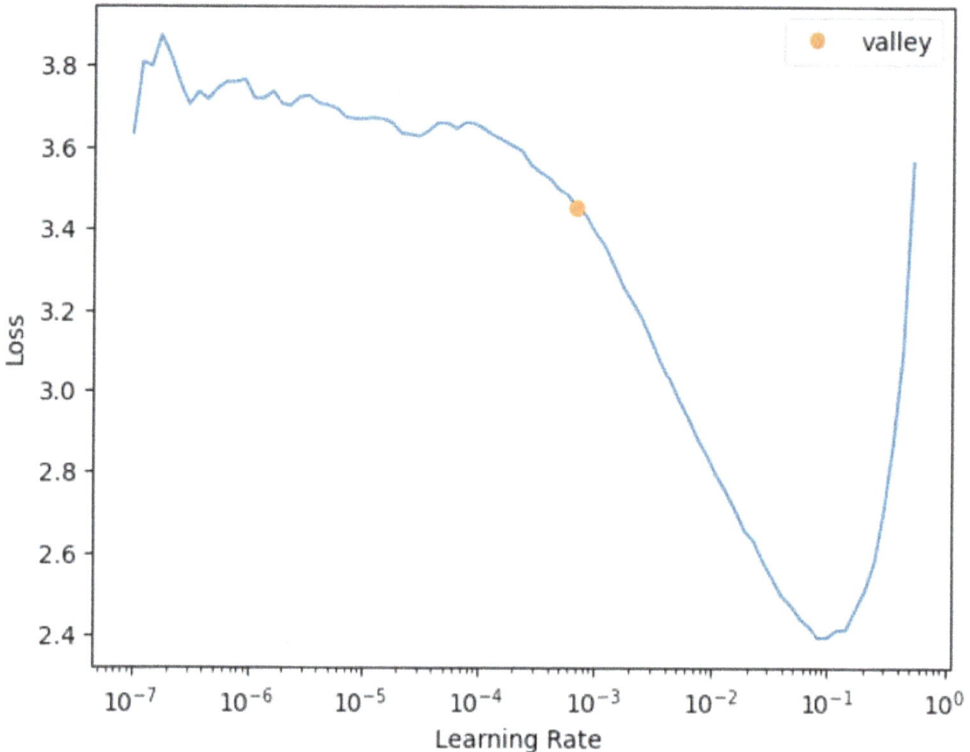

We have a plot Loss vs. Learning Rate. It is advised to select a learning rate where loss decreases. We have the suggestion from the library as an orange point. Now we can start training. Remember about overfitting and let's just train for three epochs:

learner34.fit_one_cycle(3, lr_max=slice(1e-3, 1e-2))

epoch	train_loss	valid_loss	accuracy	time
0	0.373247	0.247235	0.921083	04:24
1	0.220832	0.195339	0.933750	04:22
2	0.146618	0.144294	0.947833	04:21

We receive 94.7% accuracy - this is very good and actually, it is much better than our previous result. Note that both training loss and validation loss decrease so everything goes well.

We can repeat the process of finding a good learning rate several times.

learner34.lr_find()

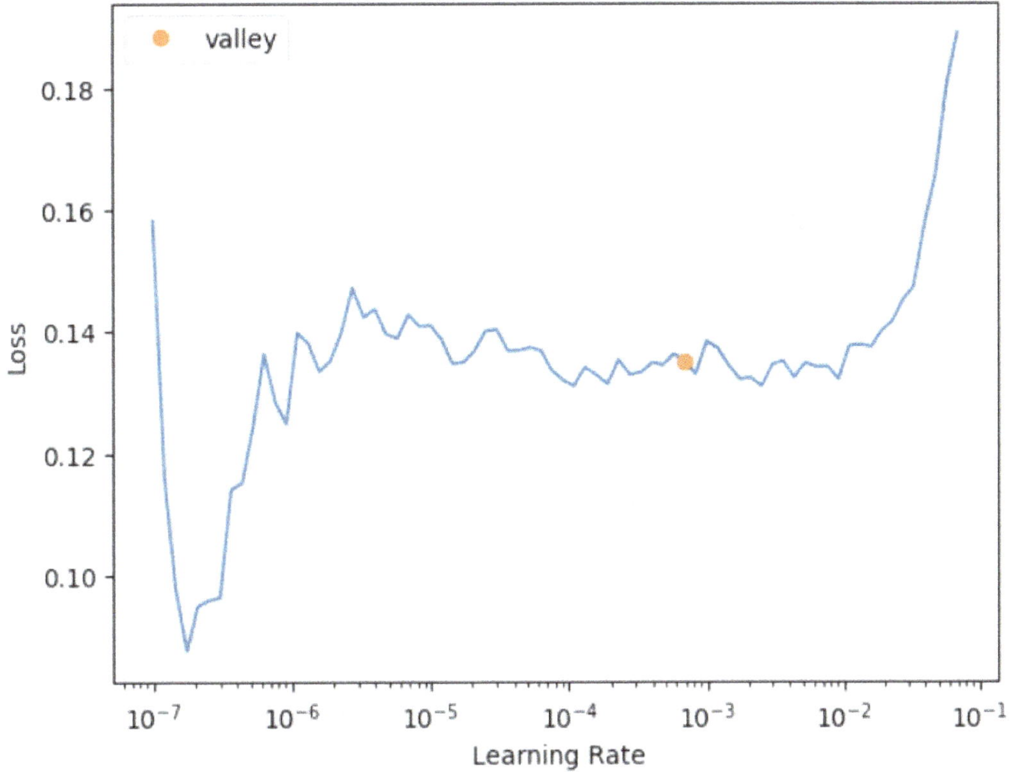

Usually during this iterative process learning rate decreases.

learner34.fit_one_cycle(2, lr_max=slice(1e-4, 1e-3))

epoch	train_loss	valid_loss	accuracy	time
0	0.130030	0.139200	0.951333	03:32
1	0.113305	0.139012	0.952750	03:30

So we just get the accuracy of 95.2% percent (and validation loss is decreasing all the time!) with such a simple code - thanks to fastai library. Let's build the confusion matrix and plot losses (feel free to compare them to similar results in our previous run):

interp34 = ClassificationInterpretation.from_learner(learner34)
interp34.plot_confusion_matrix(figsize=(13,10))

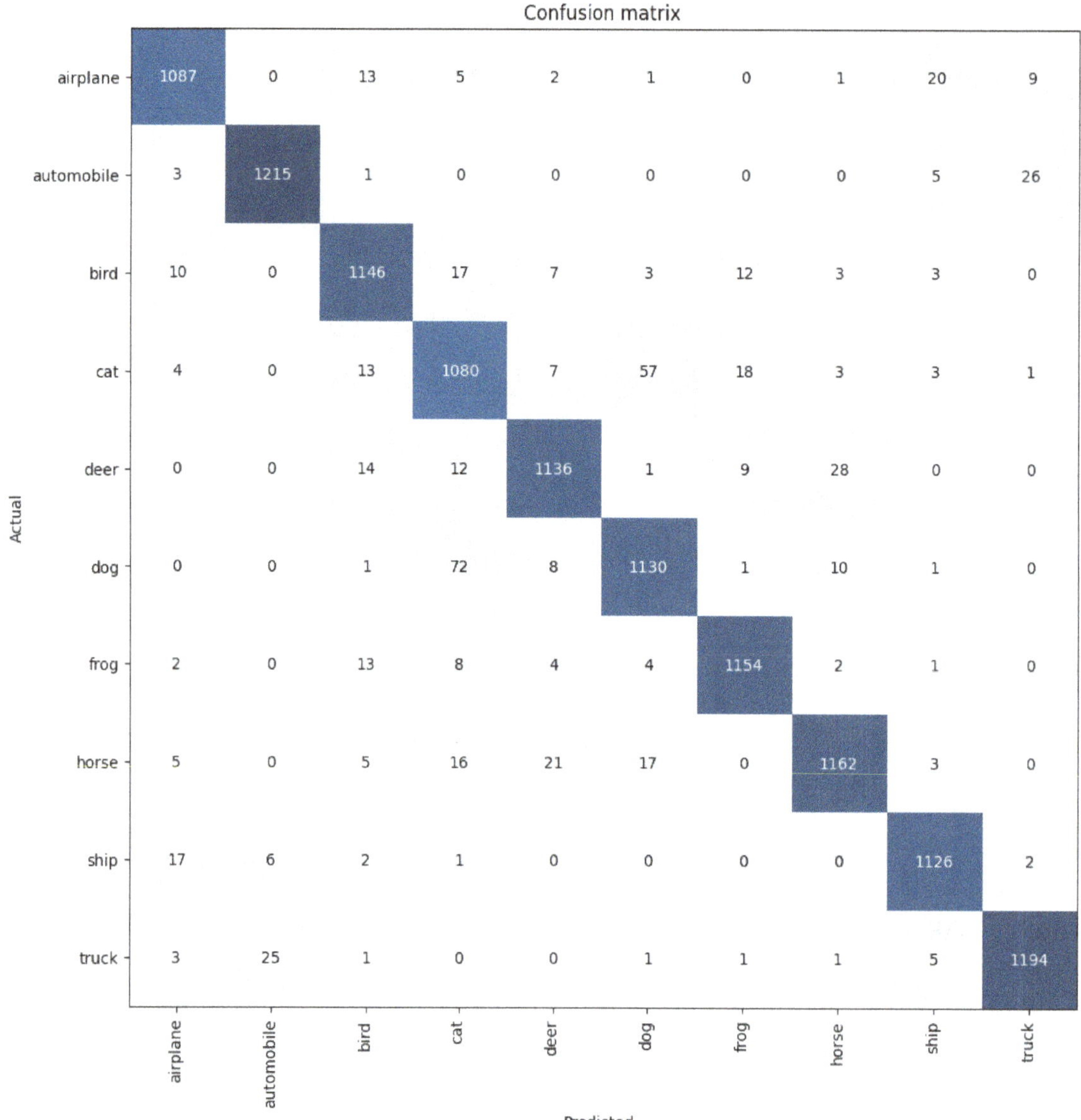

Confusion matrix

interp34.plot_top_losses(12, nrows=4, figsize=(13, 8))

You can try more iterations or epochs - just don't forget to check validation loss.

When you are done with one network, ResNet34 in our case, you can try other ResNets (ResNet18, ResNet50, etc.) or other CNN architectures.

Chapter 9. What Python is Not Good For

Throughout this book we have discussed what a great language Python is and how it could be used. But it has its own problems and disadvantages (as any other language, I believe). In this chapter, we will briefly talk about the areas where Python is not so good (or even bad or totally unsuitable).

Mobile Applications

Mobile applications have a great impact on our lives nowadays and everyone uses them. For programming languages it is also important to provide support for mobile development. For example, Kotlin became really popular when Google decided to make it a recommended language for Android.

And what about Python, it seems it is definitely not the first choice language for mobile? It is correct, there are not so many mobile applications written in Python (but worth noting that Instagram mobile application partially uses Python, specifically CPython - the default reference implementation of Python written in C of C89/C99 standard). Python hasn't got any built-in mobile modules. The main problem for Python mobile development is that it is often not fast enough for smartphones.

If you still want to create a mobile application with Python, you have a couple of options. The first is to use 3rd party mobile frameworks like Kivy or PyQt. It is a cross-platform approach that allows to support iOS and Android with one codebase. This should work for simple applications but you may encounter problems if you develop something more complex. There is no guarantee these frameworks are mature enough. The second possible approach is to develop the back-end using Python/Django and the front-end separately using some other framework.

Speed

So while talking about mobile applications we have noted that Python sometimes is not fast enough, let's discuss the problem of Python and its speed in more detail. Python is generally slower than compiled languages like C/C++ because it is an interpreted language, which means that it is interpreted during runtime instead of being compiled to native code at the time of compilation. It is also slower than interpreted languages that use JIT (just-in-time compiler) - these languages are Java and .NET - and JIT allows the compilation of byte code to native code in runtime.

SOURCE CODE   ⟶   BYTECODE   ⟶   VIRTUAL MACHINE

When we feed a source file into Python interpreter, it actually translates it into a bytecode. The bytecode is a low-level platform-independent representation of the source code, a set of instructions for Python Virtual Machine (PVM). The PVM runs the bytecode.

We have already mentioned CPython implementation and it is essential that there are different implementations of Python. CPython is the most popular of them so usually when talking about Python we mean CPython. But there is a bunch of other implementations including Jython written in Java, IronPython written in C#, PyPy written in RPython.

One of the CPython features is Python Global Interpreter Lock (GIL). It prevents multiple threads from executing Python bytecodes at once. The reason for inventing GIL was the fact that CPython memory management is not thread-safe so GIL helps to prevent race conditions. Some of the operations like input/output or Numpy processing happen outside GIL but if your program has many operations inside GIL this can degrade its performance. Some of Python implementations have GIL and some of them haven't (JPython and IronPython have no GIL, for instance).

CPython doesn't have JIT, it is difficult to create it because of its dynamic nature. It is worth mentioning that there are efforts to create JIT for CPython, for example, Numba - an open-source JIT compiler that translates a subset of Python and Numpy into fast-machine code. With Numba you can mark what source code you need to optimize. You can get great results for Numpy arrays and loops using Numba.

Finally, let's say that Python language creators are working at Python speed in the latest versions and planning to continue that. It is stated that Python 3.11 is faster by 10-60% in various tests compared to Python 3.10 and the next versions are going to be even faster. Python interpreter starts faster and core modules loading and saving are being optimized. They work at the optimization of recursive calls and function stack frames memory. The aim of the team led by Guido van Rossum is to double Python speed in the next versions.

Graphical User Interface

Python is not so good at creating graphical user interfaces. There is no one standard user interface library so it is your choice what library to use if you still need a user interface for the Python program. Options include: Tkinter which is a Python binding to the Tk GUI toolkit (rather old so your user interface is going to be quite outdated), Kivy which is mostly for mobile applications (we mentioned it earlier), PyQt and PySide which are the wrappers for Qt Framework and some other libraries.

PyQt and PySide seem to be more powerful than other available libraries. If you would like to know more about them, please address Martin Fitzpatrick's book [18].

It seems though that there is no silver bullet for creating a cross-platform interface with Python tools.

Database Management

A lot of applications in the world use databases for data storage and management. Database layer options in Python are not as powerful as in C# or Java that's why we consider it a Python disadvantage. But still, there are options to create database clients in Python, let's briefly describe them.

SQLite

Python SQLite3 module is used to integrate the SQLite database with Python. SQLite databases are convenient for the internal storage of data in your application. SQLite3 module is a standardized Python DBI API 2.0 and provides a straightforward interface for interacting with SQLite databases. Let's look at how to connect to an existing SQLite database and perform a query:

import sqlite3

conn = sqlite3.connect('test.db')

cursor = conn.execute("SELECT id, name, address, salary from EMPLOYEE")

conn.close()

This way you can perform any query, i.e. create a table, select, insert, delete a record, etc. If you modify the database (with INSERT, for instance), you should call **conn.commit()** to commit the transaction.

Python SQLite3 module may be a good choice for a small application database but this approach is not suitable for a large concurrent database.

ODBC

It is possible to work with ODBC (Open Database Connectivity) databases like SQL Server, MySQL or Oracle using pyodbc package (you need Python 3.7 or later for full support). First, it is necessary to install the package:

>pip install pyodbc

Then we can connect to a database and perform a query as we did for SQLite.

```
import pyodbc
conn = pyodbc.connect("Driver={SQL Server Native Client 11.0};"
            "Server=server_name;"
            "Database=db_name;"
            "Trusted_Connection=yes;")

cursor = conn.cursor()
cursor.execute('SELECT * FROM Table')

cursor.close()
conn.close()
```

Queries syntax is not checked from the Python side so you have to check their correctness separately. It may be not convenient for complex queries.

SQLAlchemy

SQLAlchemy is the Python SQL toolkit and Object Relational Mapper (ORM). ORM is what SQLAlchemy so important, with it you can map classes into the database. SQLAlchemy supports many popular databases including SQLite, Microsoft SQL Server, Oracle and PostgreSQL.

You can install it like this:

>pip install sqlalchemy

We won't describe SQLAlchemy, just show how the mapping of classes can be done.

```
class Employee(Base):
    __tablename__ = 'employees'
    id=Column(Integer, primary_key=True)
    first_name=Column('first_name', String(32))
    last_name=Column('last_name', String(32))
    worked_hours=Column('hours', Integer)
    salary=Column(salary, Numeric)
```

Here we map Employee class into **'employees'** database table specifying the fields mapping into database columns.

It is possible to specify different types of relationships in a database using SQLAlchemy.

About Myself

When I studied in university, my major was theoretical physics so my first programs were for numerical simulations of various physical processes. I used Maple or MATLAB packages for this purpose and also wrote small programs using Pascal and C++.

After university I became a software developer instead of a physicist and after using C++ for several years switched to C# and .NET world in order to create more complex applications dealing with enterprise, complex business logic, and databases. I lived happily with C# using it from .NET Framework 1.1 to current .NET 7 but several years ago I became interested in deep learning stuff. Since the majority of libraries in the world of machine and deep learning use Python and I started to use it and found it great for many things, not only related to deep learning but in other areas as well.

In parallel I used Go for other projects and found it a great tool for its own area as well (maybe I should write another book about Go?).

So my personal experience led me to what I tried to explain in this book: there is no universal language for all programming purposes or tasks. You need to consider various approaches and different programming languages to select the one that fits your area and needs.

References

[0] https://www.python.org/

[1] Paul Barry. Head First Python 2e: A Brain-Friendly Guide.
https://www.amazon.co.uk/dp/1491919531

[2] Eric Matthes. Python Crash Course, 3rd Edition: A Hands-On, Project-Based Introduction to Programming. https://www.amazon.co.uk/dp/1718502702

[3] https://www.coursera.org/specializations/python

[4] Ryan Michell. Web Scraping with Python: Collecting More Data from the Modern Web.
https://www.amazon.com/_/dp/1491985577?smid=ATVPDKIKX0DER&_encoding=UTF8&tag=oreilly20-20

[5] https://openai.com/

[6] https://matplotlib.org

[7] Nicolas P. Rougier. Scientific Visualization: Python + Matplotlib.
 https://github.com/rougier/scientific-visualization-book

[8] https://opencv.org/

[9] https://en.wikipedia.org/wiki/OCR-A

[10] https://scikit-learn.org/

[11] http://archive.ics.uci.edu/dataset/53/iris

[12] https://en.wikipedia.org/wiki/AlexNet

[13] https://www.tensorflow.org/

[14] https://pytorch.org/

[15] https://www.fast.ai/

[16] https://www.cs.toronto.edu/~kriz/cifar.html

[17] https://colab.research.google.com/

[18] Martin Fitzpatrick. Create GUI applications with Python and Qt6
https://www.pythonguis.com/pyside6-book/